MUDHOLE SMITH

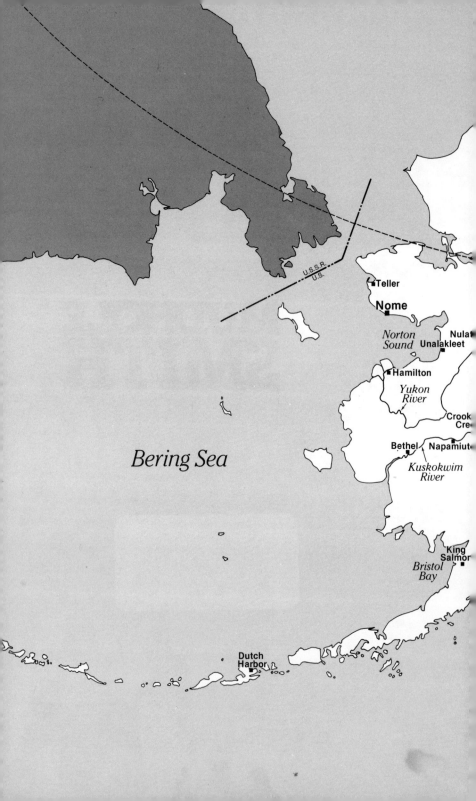

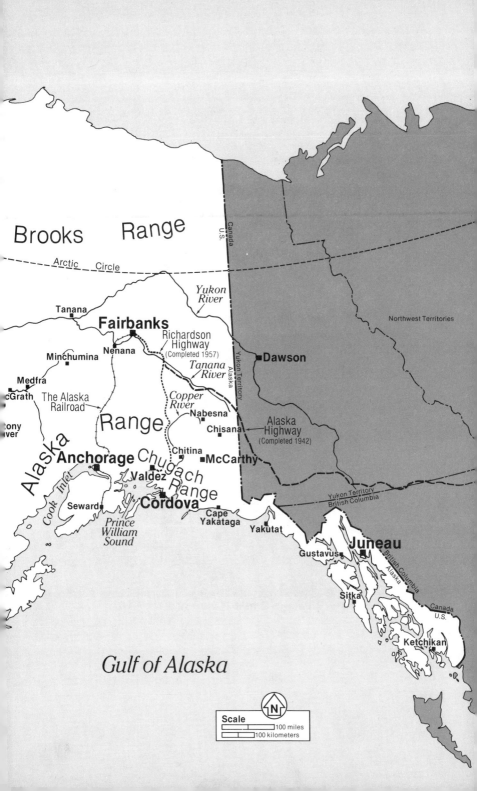

Brooks   Range

Arctic   Circle

Yukon River

Tanana   **Fairbanks**

Richardson
Highway
(Completed 1957)

Canada
U.S.

Nenana

Minchumina

Tanana River

Medfra

The Alaska
Railroad

cGrath

Dawson

Northwest Territories

Copper River

Range

Nabesna

ony
ver

Chisana

Yukon Territory
Alaska

Alaska
Highway
(Completed 1942)

Chitina

Anchorage   Chugach

McCarthy

Alaska

Valdez

Range

Cook Inlet

Seward

Cordova

Cape
Yakataga

Yukon Territory
British Columbia

Prince William Sound

Yakutat

Juneau

Gustavus

British Columbia
Alaska

Sitka

Canada
U.S.

Gulf of Alaska

Ketchikan

Scale
☐☐☐☐100 miles
☐☐☐☐100 kilometers

Merle "Mudhole" Smith. (Courtesy of the FAA)

MUDHOLE SMITH

Alaska Flier

Lone E. Janson

ALASKA NORTHWEST
PUBLISHING COMPANY
Anchorage, Alaska

All photographs are courtesy of Merle Smith unless otherwise noted.

First Printing: 1981
Third Printing: 1985

Library of Congress cataloging in publication data:
Janson, Lone E.
   Mudhole Smith, Alaska flier.
   1. Smith, Merle K.   2. Air pilots—Alaska—
Biography.   I. Title.
TL540.S646J36   629.13'092'4   [B]   81-4529
ISBN 0-88240-139-4   AACR2

Design by Jon.Hersh
The cover: illustration by Val Paul Taylor;
the plane is the *Yellow Peril,* drawn from the actual Boeing 80-A
flown by Mudhole Smith and other Alaska pilots and now a part of the
Pacific Museum of Flight aircraft collection.

Alaska Northwest Publishing Company
Box 4-EEE, Anchorage, Alaska 99509

Printed in U.S.A.

For anyone who has ever spent a winter in Alaska's bush there can be only one possible dedication for this book — to those pilots who bring food, mail, medical help, news and gossip. To the guy with the most welcome set of wings in the world, the Alaska bush pilot.

CONTENTS

Foreword

"So you're writing a book about Mudhole Smith? Let *me* write a chapter!" I heard that several times in Cordova when the word of the project got out. It was assurance that here was a colorful character whose life really was worth a book.

In a typical anecdote they tell about the time Smitty and a group of cohorts were in Washington, D.C., trying to get the federal government to understand the problems of Alaska. In one of the lulls between hearings, they wound up in a fancy restaurant for dinner. The place had everything: candles, wine and a strolling violinist. His mind on business, Smitty was driving home a point in the discussion. At his elbow the violinist was pouring forth sweet music in direct competition. At last Mudhole could stand it no longer. "How can a person talk with that caterwauling going on?" he roared. The violinist folded his bow and departed.

The famous Mudhole temperament came from three decades of fighting some of the cussedest weather on the North American continent; flying where you need wheels, skis and pontoons, sometimes all in the same flight; where the fog comes and goes like a yo-yo, and where the clouds often have rocks in them. With all that, a man could hardly be expected to come through even-tempered.

My first contact with Smitty came when he carried me on his back out to his plane. A girl friend and I were weathered in for five days at Valdez, waiting to get to Cordova, before the little pontoon plane could come in for a landing on Valdez Bay. We went down to the water's edge, but neither of us had hip boots so Smitty wound up carrying us both on his back out to the plane. Such is the life of a bush pilot.

I learned, in those early days in Alaska, how it was to live in isolated places and depend on that little bush airplane. When Cordova Air arrived once a month, it meant fresh meat, fresh groceries, mail, news, parcels ordered months before from Sears, and local gossip from town. At Katalla the plane landed across Katalla Slough on the hard-packed sand. We all waited on the beach while someone took a skiff across the slough and picked up the mail sacks and grocery orders. It was like Christmas every month.

The floating cannery, too, was a place where we waited for the mail plane. It came several times a week, and it was as exciting as it had been in Katalla. Sometimes I even swam out to the plane after the prop stopped turning.

The excitement and anticipation were only part of it; there was always the knowledge that in case of sickness or accident, a radio call would bring a plane. When there are no doctors about, that's reassuring. Sometimes the plane landed in abominable weather. Alaska's bush pilots are incredible people. They always have been and still are.

I remember waiting at the Cordova airport in Bob Korn's cold drafty bus, because there was no terminal building at the time. I remember Smitty's DC3's and a number of trips to Anchorage in them. The stewardess always brought passengers a blanket as a matter of course. Airplanes were not comfortably warm.

Later, in the new terminal, a group of us were kidding Smitty about Cordova Airlines. Frank Theodore told Smitty with a straight face, "Every airplane you've got was shot down in World War II!" Alaskan humor spares no one.

And, oh yes, there was my first "Champagne Flight" on any airline. It was aboard Cordova Airlines' new Convair to Juneau in the mid-1960s. I thought a champagne flight meant one glass of champagne. When the stewardess came down the aisle with the second round, I supposed that since the plane wasn't very full, she had some left over and, I was in luck because I got a second glass.

When she came down the aisle a third time, it dawned on me that by a champagne flight, they meant nonstop champagne. I had a third glass. By the time we landed at Yakutat, halfway to Juneau, I was flying higher than the airplane.

I lived in Cordova for about thirty years. All that time I never knew that Smitty and his buddies had built their own plane and then proceeded to teach themselves to fly it. I had no idea that the Mudhole Smith of my acquaintance was once an honest-to-goodness barnstormer and stunt flier in aerial circuses.

I learned about that when I was asked to cover the story of "Mudhole Smith Day," the civic bash Cordova put on for Mudhole after his retirement. Smitty showed me his display of aerial circus posters, old pictures and even the rope ladder they had used. That's when I knew I had to write this book.

— Lone Janson

Special thanks to the following in addition to those mentioned in the book: Lyle Barron, Glen Henderson, Max Metcalf, Bud Hill, my brother Paul R. Smith, sister Hilda Richardson, cousin Don Smith, Irwin Knoepl, Sam Murphy, Frank Post, Charlie Schianost, and my cousin Dean Smith.

These people would help with little or no pay, just for the fun and sheer love of flying.

Then there is my mom and dad, Russell and Mary Smith, who didn't care much for the idea of my being a flier, but who helped me and encouraged me anyway.

— *Merle K. "Mudhole" Smith*

MERLE'S YOUTH IN THE MIDWEST

A Fly-Crazy Kid

"Learn to fly!" urged the ad. "Learn to fly on the ground — no need to have an airplane!"

Thirteen-year-old Merle Smith studied the ad closely. It was from an aircraft company; it pictured a set of "controls" which could be bolted to any surface and allow a person to actually get the feel of flying — or at least so said the ad.

It was the early 1920s. Barnstorming was coming to its height and air mail was being pioneered. Every boy's mind was set afire with stories of the great aviation feats of World War I — the Sopwith Camels, the Spads and Jennies; "Curse you, Red Baron!" and all that. It was the day of open cockpits, goggles and streaming neck scarves.

Kansas, where Smitty lived, was one of the cradles of the infant aviation industry. The flat lands and fields made great landing places. Pilots hung around the barns and fields telling stories of flying adventure. Young Merle Smith hung around them, listening and dreaming of flight. He couldn't remember when he didn't want to fly.

The first time he ever heard an airplane was when he was sitting in a schoolroom in Gallia, Kansas. The kids were having trouble studying because they could hear this awful roaring. It was a time when tractors were first coming into use, and they were a great curiosity.

"If somebody had a tractor," recalled Smitty, "you'd go for miles to see them plowing. They were mostly those old Mogul tractors; they had one cylinder and you could hear them for a hundred miles and when you stood up in the cab they'd raise you six inches off the floor every time they'd fire, so I knew this engine we heard in class wasn't a tractor.

"I kept trying to crane my neck out the window, and the teacher bawled me out but good, and all the time my father, who had a field right across the road from the schoolhouse, was yelling at the top of his lungs. He was trying to get us to come out and see the airplane flying over.

"That night when I got home my father told me what we had missed. I was certainly mad at that teacher."

During World War I Smitty was just big enough to read the papers a little, but he followed the exploits of the flying aces. He read all about Capt. Eddie Rickenbacker, and the news that the ex-president's son, Kermit Roosevelt, was shot down.

It wasn't till after World War I that he actually saw an airplane in flight; they were still that rare. In 1921 a barnstormer by the name of Preacher Smith came through the area with a Jenny and put on a small aerial circus performance.

Preacher Smith was a former World War I pilot out of Chanute, Kansas, the son of a preacher. He would never fly on Sunday. Not flying on Sunday was a true financial sacrifice, since a pilot could often make up to five hundred dollars on that one day. So you could say that Preacher Smith truly had the courage of his convictions.

The Saturday that Preacher Smith flew near Colony, Kansas, young Merle sat all day in the field and watched him fly. And when he could bear it no longer he went home to the farm where he had a number of sheep of his own, and he took his favorite sheep, the one he loved the most, and sold her for $10. Smitty took $7.50 of that $10 to Preacher Smith and bought his first airplane ride.

The farmer Merle sold his sheep to realized how much the boy loved the animal, so he later allowed him to work two weeks to redeem his pet.

So Merle had experienced flight, and was filled with a yearning to fly. But yearning and learning were two different matters. Flying instruction was difficult and expensive to obtain. In all the United States, Merle was able to learn of only two flying schools, and he wrote eager letters to both of them. The first was a school in Minneola, New York, run by the Curtiss-Wright Company. They replied with a long letter and several brochures, which the fly-crazy youth read avidly over and over again for descriptions of soaring in the wild blue yonder. But the gist of it was that he could probably be soloed in a month or two for the sum of not less than three thousand dollars. That much money could buy a whole township in eastern Kansas.

After receiving four or five letters from Smitty, the other school wrote back a short, curt note, which plainly conveyed that they weren't too interested in enrolling the lad as a student. They probably guessed that he had no money and was only fishing.

For those who couldn't afford lessons, it was almost impossible to learn to fly. Their only alternative was to join a flying circus, and even that offered little actual time in the air. A kid named Cloyce Anderson, from Lone Elm, about five miles from Smitty's home town of Colony, took a job as "grease monkey-flunky," traveling with Preacher Smith for a full summer. Cloyce had hoped to get at least a few hours in the air, but the only time the plane was not in use for profit was when they were traveling to another town. Then the front cockpit, where Cloyce rode as a passenger, was piled so high with such accessories as gas cans, water cans and spare parts that Preacher Smith did not hook up the controls. At other times Cloyce did not even get to fly between towns. He was transported in a car.

Hearing all this, Merle was as disappointed as Cloyce. The only avenue to flight experience that seemed open offered very little flying. So, when Smitty saw the ad for the flight controls that promised you could "learn to fly" on the ground, he was quick to send off for the kit.

The Kansas farmhouse of the Russell Smith family had a huge, wrap-around porch, and after much begging, Merle's father allowed him to bolt the apparatus to the porch floor. Young Merle practiced by the hour. His dad figured it was a harmless enough pastime, so he'd smile tolerantly and shake his head when the boy sat there going "brr-rroom" and working his controls as he dreamed of flying.

A neighbor boy was just as crazy about tractors as Merle was about airplanes. Both machines were new enough to have a certain glamor to them. The kid down the road fixed up a bent stick for a steering wheel and he'd "drive" down the dusty country lanes roaring "brr-room, brr-room" like a tractor. People put up with him, figuring he just wasn't all there.

One day Merle's father, Russell, was outside the barber shop in Colony. The barber shop was the neighborhood gathering place where news and gossip of the week was exchanged. Those inside did not see Russell standing outside, and he happened to overhear their conversation.

"Between that crazy kid and his tractors, and the Smith boy and his airplanes. . . ." Smith didn't wait to hear more. With the laughter of his friends ringing in his ears he stormed home, ripped up Merle's "learn to fly" controls and threw them out. And that was the last of that.

In 1923 another barnstormer came through Smitty's part of the country. B.T. Barber was a Ford dealer in Iola, and his brother ran the Ford garage in Colony. One fine Sunday B.T. brought his Curtiss Oriole to Colony and offered rides to one and all for $2.50 apiece.

Young Merle was able to get his second airplane ride at that time and was greatly impressed by the Curtiss Oriole.

"The difference between a Jenny and an Oriole," he said, "was the difference between a Model T and a Packard. The Oriole had beautiful wings, not strung with as many wires as a Jenny, and it hauled two passengers in the front seat. My new ambition was to own a Curtiss Oriole."

There still seemed to be no way of getting time in the air except to work with a flying circus, as his friend Cloyce had done, and take his chances. Next spring Merle left school early and went with a barnstormer from western Kansas who had an old J-1 Standard. Smitty sold tickets and did flunky work, hoping to get a chance at the controls in the forward cockpit, but his luck was no better than his friend Cloyce. He went back to high school the next fall, still disappointed. But there he met a friend who had an airplane — Duard Murray and his wonderful flying machine, the *Murray Sport.*

The Murray Sport

It was a beautiful machine; at least to young Merle Smith's eyes. Duard Murray and another boy named Herb Henderson had acquired the fuselage of a World War I fighter plane that had been cracked up at the Iola Fair. The plane had nosed over on landing and bent the crankshaft, in effect ruining the entire engine. Herb and Duard had bought the wreck for fifty dollars.

Duard was a year ahead of Smitty in high school, and Herb Henderson a few years older yet. Herb worked in a bank, and to the boys this meant he had access to money. He didn't, of course, but at least he had a job and it was mostly his money that financed the acquisition of the plane and a brand new 88-hp LeRhone engine, which the two older boys had found at an aircraft factory in Lawrence, Kansas.

During the rebuilding of the plane Murray displayed a natural talent for aeronautical engineering. He streamlined the fuselage and replaced the double bays with a single bay; that is, he eliminated many of the struts and wires that cluttered the wings of the original design.

Smitty was so interested in airplanes he couldn't stay away from the rebuilding activities. He spent almost all his spare time there, and he and Duard became fast friends.

The original airplane had been equipped with only a 60- or 65-hp Gnome engine, so the newer, more powerful 88-hp LeRhone really "souped up" the little plane. The boys took their creation out onto the Kansas farm fields and taxied around to get the feel of it. There was no question whether it would fly; it was hot enough that it would have jumped right off the ground and gone up fast, but the boys held it down, feeling the plane out. First one would try it, then the next one. They'd taxi around in big circles, and sometimes they would run into things and damage the plane with its fragile woodwork and fabric materials. Then they'd have to rebuild it.

At first Duard and Henderson did all the taxiing. As partners with a financial interest in the plane, they felt they had the right, but finally they let the younger boy, Merle, try it. Smitty did a few times, but there was something about the little plane that unnerved him, although he couldn't explain what it was. Looking back, he realized it was the sheer power of the plane. Although he stayed with it a while longer, Herb Henderson began to lose interest in the plane. "Herb had a job, and he already knew there were better ways to make a living," Smitty laughed.

Duard and Merle spent most of the following winter repairing the plane from various damages. During this rebuilding, Merle began putting what little money he could scrape up into the enterprise.

The next spring the *Murray Sport* was again ready to fly, and they took it out into the pastures for some more sky-hooting around. Neither of them could work up enough courage to take the plane off the ground, though they were to the stage of skimming along at grass height.

One day after practicing all morning in a cow pasture, they went to town for a quick lunch. Town was only a short distance, and they probably weren't gone over an hour.

When they came back they were utterly dismayed. The cows were eating the fabric off the wings.

With cries of anger and distress, they chased the cows away and surveyed the damage. Not only had the cows eaten most of the fabric off the wings, they had used the fragile woodwork as a back-scratching tool, and the plane was as demolished as if it had been crashed.

They spent most of the summer rebuilding the plane, then went back to the pasture. It was a huge field, and right through the middle of it ran the old Santa Fe Trail to Kansas City and Santa Fe. In the early twenties, the ruts were still two and three feet deep where the wagons had passed and they spread over a wide area, a hundred feet or more.

The boys didn't dare to hit the ruts, but by this time they were getting the feel of the plane. They would run it down to the ruts, then skim over them at grass height. After they were across they would coast to a stop. Then they did it all over again.

Duard, especially, was feeling encouraged. They'd take the plane to the north end of the field, and Duard would get in the pilot's cockpit in back. While he was climbing in, Herb would say, "Now go ahead and take 'er off this time! Go ahead and do it!" Smitty and Herb patted Duard on the back, telling him he could do it if he tried. A set expression would come into Duard's face, and then he'd grit his teeth and start out. When he reached the Santa Fe Trail ruts, he'd skim across the grass and coast to a stop.

After about eight or ten tries, Duard started down the field with a mighty roar and lifted her off. As soon as he got into the air he was in trouble. His right wing went down, and though he had practiced endlessly, excitement robbed him of his memory. He couldn't think of what to do to get that wing up. The plane hit the ground, smashing the woodwork and tearing the fabric. Duard was shaken but safe.

Duard and Smitty rebuilt the plane. They were not learning much about flying, but they were at least gaining a good experience in aircraft repair and maintenance. The rib-stitching, taping, application of fabric and all the other details were becoming abundantly familiar.

Duard Murray was the real designer of the *Murray Sport*, and several local pilots seemed interested in it even though the plane had never flown. Duard was a natural aeronautical engineer, and his interests tended toward building planes, while young Smitty thought of nothing but flying.

After the *Sport* was rebuilt this time, an individual appeared who said he was a World War I sergeant, which apparently he had been. He also said he could fly, a statement the boys accepted willingly enough because Duard so fervently wanted to see the plane tested in the air. The ex-sergeant easily talked them into letting him take up the *Murray Sport*.

They went to a field about seven miles west of Colony. It was a big one, about ten times what was needed to get the *Sport* off the ground.

The sergeant climbed in and roared down the field. The boys saw immediately that the man knew little or nothing about flying. He started off with a stiff cross-wind, and in those days you simply didn't do that.

But it was too late. The sergeant stayed on the ground at full throttle, far beyond what was needed to take off. Still he kept rolling. At the far end of the field was a sturdy fence made of deeply-set posts, barbed wire and thorn hedging. Into the fence the sergeant plowed the *Murray Sport*, and it was demolished again.

The sergeant walked away and the boys never saw him again.

They contemplated the wreckage of their little plane and gave serious thought to going somewhere and finding a job, maybe in one of the airplane plants nearby, with the idea of learning to fly on the side.

In May of 1924, Duard and Merle left home and drove to Lincoln, Nebraska, where they visited the Lincoln Standard Aircraft Company plant. In Smitty's mind, that was when he really got serious about flying. He had been fooling around for two or three years with the *Murray Sport*, but now he decided that come what may, this move was it.

Duard and Merle met the president of the Lincoln Standard plant, Ray Page. Page was an excellent pilot in his own right, and Charles Lindbergh had taken a few flying lessons at the plant the year before. However, Lindbergh was apparently having the same problem as all aspiring pilots; it cost so much a man could fly only a day or two, then he'd have to work for a month or more to afford another day or two. So Lindbergh joined a flying circus as a parachutist.

It took Page a very short time to discover that the two boys had a better than average knowledge of aircraft maintenance and repair. He was desperate for such people. He took them on a tour of the aircraft factory and showed them some of the new planes. One in particular caught Smitty's eye. It was an LS-5, an open cockpit job that carried four passengers in the forward cockpit. Two of the passengers' seats faced forward, two backward. The plane was powered by a 180-hp Hispano-Suiza engine. There were several of them and Page said they were all sold.

"Rich people," he explained. "Race horse owners down in the bluegrass country. They want to ride around in the planes, but they don't want to fly them. We could send them out today if we could get pilots for them."

The two young men examined the classy airplanes, their eyes shining, and hearts pumping wildly to think of being able to take such a job. But neither of them could fly, and Page wanted them to work in the factory with a vague promise of learning to fly "sometime." Still, it seemed to be the only thing open with any promise of future flight, so they accepted the job Page offered.

The plant manager gave them the names and addresses of several good rooming houses where they could stay cheaply and eat well. They drove off to look for living accommodations.

As they pulled up in front of the first address on their list, Murray shut off the engine of the car, but he didn't get out right away. He had a thoughtful look in his eye.

Smitty had climbed out of the Model T, but he paused there and waited for Murray to speak.

"You know what I'm thinking?" Duard said slowly. "I'm thinking if we take this job, we'll probably be here the rest of our lives."

Smitty thought it over for a moment and agreed.

Murray said firmly, "I'm not going to."

Smitty asked, "What are you going to do?"

"I'm going to go back and get the old *Sport* going. I think that's more what I want to do."

So Smitty got back in the car and closed the door. "I'll go with you," he said, and the two drove back to the aircraft plant and told Mr. Page they were going back and rebuild their own airplane, and that they'd see him in a couple of months.

They drove back to Colony never returning to take the jobs at the Lincoln Standard plant.

Flight at Last

When Duard and Smitty came back from Lincoln to their wrecked plane, Duard, the older of the two, decided to move the craft to a town where there was an airfield, and rebuild it under the watchful eye of some experienced pilots. In the winter of 1924-25 he took the *Murray Sport* to Iola, Kansas.

There, at last, the plane became airborne. Fritz Womack, who had helped build the Iola airport, first flew the *Murray Sport* in the spring of 1925. During the winter he had given instructions in flying to Duard, first in his own Jenny, and by spring Duard was ready for the *Murray Sport*. Duard soloed in it and began flying the *Sport* around the country.

He soon got a job in an aircraft factory in Kansas City, and married. Smitty, meanwhile, was finishing high school. Duard came down on weekends to give him instructions in flying.

The drive from Kansas City to Colony was a long one, and

Duard's new wife was not too happy about losing their weekends together. She soon gave Duard the word: either finish off Smitty's lessons as soon as possible, or else.

So Duard told Smitty, "Well, you're not ready to solo, but you're not going to kill yourself, either." And Smitty, confident as all fledglings that he was long since ready to go it alone, took off and soloed at last.

By this time Smitty had made a deal to buy out the other partners' interest in the *Murray Sport* for two hundred dollars and a car. Duard, as the designer, wanted to build more of the planes. Fritz Womack was to be a partner in this endeavor.

Both Duard and Smitty were close to dead broke, but the bargain was struck, and to celebrate Smitty's solo they went downtown for a bowl of chili. Duard told Smitty that he might have trouble making money with the *Sport*, because it wasn't the type for barnstorming. It was unsuited for aerobatics and was limited in passenger capacity.

They discussed this for a while, but Merle felt he had no real choice. He needed money, both to buy the plane and to make a living. He *had* to fly passengers.

Before leaving for Kansas City, Duard wanted to take his wife up for one last jaunt in the little plane, so the two of them took off. As they returned to the field, the engine quit. Duard was able to make a dead stick landing, but he told Smitty not to fly until the engine was overhauled.

Smitty spent the next five days working on the engine and finished the job before the weekend. He was now ready for the big adventure. He recruited a young fellow from Colony to help him as flunky and ticketseller, and the two of them took off early Sunday morning for the little town of LeRoy about fifteen miles away.

As was the custom for barnstormers, he flew down over the town, circling and racing his engine. It was all the notice needed to bring out people to buy airplane rides. Then he flew to a huge 720-acre field just north of LeRoy, which was perfect for his purpose. He landed and was ready for business, at two dollars a ride.

Soon a young fellow arrived in a Model T and Smitty took him up for an uneventful spin around the country. As he set the airplane down in the field, another car came driving up with a whole load of fellows anxious to ride in an airplane.

Smitty knew one of the men. Afraid that if he were recognized nobody would ride with him, he remained in the pilot's seat in the after cockpit with his helmet and goggles on and his face averted.

The man who knew Smitty was a big fellow, an auctioneer named Jess Holmes. He and another young man approached the plane.

Jess asked, "How long you been flying, son?"

"Ten years," Smitty lied. This answer seemed to satisfy Holmes. The younger man said to Holmes, "I'd like to go up, but I don't want to ride alone."

Holmes agreed. "Yeah. I don't want to go up alone either. How about our going together?"

"There's only one seat," Smitty pointed out.

"Well, how about if we sort of squeeze in? My friend is pretty small."

Smitty looked them over. Jess Holmes probably weighed close to 200 pounds, and his buddy 120. The total weight was pretty heavy, but he didn't want to argue for fear Holmes would recognize him.

"Well, if you can both get in there, okay. But it ain't built for two; there's no room."

Both men climbed in, and the younger one sat on Holmes' lap. Their heads stuck up a foot above the forward cockpit windshield, but Smitty was committed to taking them.

He signaled his helper, who cranked the prop. Smitty taxied to one corner of the field and headed diagonally across the pasture to be sure he had plenty of room to get off with the extra weight.

The little plane hopped off the ground and climbed to about 150 feet. That was as high as it would go, the absolute ceiling. Some of the trees along the Neosho River looked higher than that as Smitty headed out over the water. He could almost feel the wheels going through their leaves, but he was able to clear them successfully and get over the river.

He wanted desperately to gain altitude. To do that he needed more speed. He put the nose down to accelerate then pulled back to climb. Again he got to 150 feet and could go no higher.

He wanted to get back to the field, but he was afraid to put a wing down to make a turn. The extra weight might just send the plane out of control.

He settled for such a wide turn he didn't have to bank at all. Some five miles later he was finally headed back to the pasture, where he landed.

"It was the first load I'd flown in that airplane," he said, describing the incident. "It just wasn't built for it. Everything worked perfect; the day was perfect, the wind was perfect, the field was perfect, or I'd never have made it. When I got back on the ground I was a little shook, but I had six dollars."

As his passengers climbed out and Smitty silently thanked his lucky stars, all the bystanders gathered around.

"Hey, my buddy and I want to go up, too."

To his horror, Smitty realized that they all wanted to ride two at a time!

This was too much for the young pilot, who had just soloed the Sunday before. He said, "You know, this engine doesn't sound exactly right. I think I'll take it up and check it out."

The crowd murmured approval of his sensible caution.

Smitty's young helper had climbed up on the wing. Smitty muttered to him, "Get in here, quick. We're leaving."

The youngster was startled. "What about our stuff?" The gas cans, water cans and other gear were still on the field.

"Forget the stuff," snapped Smitty. The helper climbed into the forward cockpit.

"Where you going, kid?" demanded one of the waiting passengers.

"I'm a mechanic," the helper said, "I've got to go along and listen to this engine."

Smitty took off. They never stopped until they got to Colony. They came back in the middle of the night with a Model T and picked up their gear.

Smitty had learned his lesson. From that time on, he flew only one passenger at a time in the *Murray Sport.*

For about a year Merle flew the plane around the country, trying to scrape together a little money. He was limited to small town celebrations and fairs because he couldn't do any aerobatics. Aerobatics were the heart of the aerial circus; a pilot who could do slow rolls, falling leafs, loops, snap rolls, and the like, could work the larger county and state fairs where the money was. He could hire a parachute jumper and maybe a stunt man who was a wing-walker, and get paid for the performance. He also could keep whatever he made hauling passengers, which was considerable at the larger fairs.

At the heart of aerial acrobatics, the stunt that really set the blood of the crowds pounding and loosened their wallets to go on flights, was the tailspin. Tailspins were exciting, vivid, dangerous — everything the crowds wanted to see. Deliberate spins from a high altitude were reasonably safe because there was plenty of time to recover.

Modern planes recover by themselves from a tailspin, and they actually have to be forced to spin at all. The old-time planes were spin-prone and killed many a pilot.

"You'd feel them sort of 'mush down' and wallow around a bit," said Smitty, "and then you were in a tailspin." Learning to spin a plane and recover it was a survival technique. Mastered, it was also good money to a barnstormer.

Whenever he could that year, Smitty hung around the Iola airport where the older pilots were always generous and willing to help the young ones. He took lessons when he could afford them. Some of the pilots refused money for their help, others worked on credit. To this day, Smitty is not sure if some of them ever were paid off.

There was Ross Arbuckle, who gave Smitty lessons in aerobatic technique, and Fritz Womack, who taught him spins and how to get out of trouble. Others Smitty remembers as being kind and helpful were B.T. Barber and Todd Toby; Ernie Bergman, owner of the airport, who let Smitty use his hangar; D.W. Yokum, Raymond Kedrick and Harry King, who overhauled his first OX-5 engine for him.

The old pilots were a fraternity, extra helpful to neophytes because they remembered the difficulties of learning to fly all too well. They provided Smitty with an informal ground school, in the time he spent just sitting around on a Saturday or Sunday under the wing of an airplane, listening to the pilots exchange stories. Many were related for amusement value, but an even greater number constituted the sharing of experience — a learning from one another of the hard lessons of flight in the infancy of the industry. It was actually the finest ground school training available for a young pilot who paid close attention and remembered what he heard.

Young Merle was all ears.

Tailspin

A burst of laughter rocked the little group of pilots clustered in the shade of the hangar. They were swapping stories, and next to actual flying, their yarns were the most enjoyable activity of all, Merle thought. The subject of the conversation happened to be tailspins, and Merle grinned as he noticed that you could almost always tell who had been a World War I trainer pilot by his crooked nose. Those who survived had broken noses or other scars as mementos of spins their students had got into at low altitude, before the instructor could recover the controls.

The pilot speaking had a long nose which took a hard turn to the left halfway down and finished decidedly off-center. "I had this student up in my Jenny," he recalled. "Before I knew what happened, he had us in a spin. It was pretty close to the ground and I didn't have time to take over. Don't know how we got out of that crack-up, but all I got was a busted nose. The kid wound up with a sprained ankle and a sore neck. Just lucky, I guess."

Raymond Kedrick said, "I saw Clarence Norton recover a plane from a low-altitude spin at Independence." The remark, delivered quietly and casually, captured the interest of the fliers. They all knew that Kansas airport surrounded by rolling hills. A flier would make his run and lift off from the crest of one of the hills. It was considered a good airport in those days.

Clarence Norton, Kedrick said, was giving lessons to a student pilot and they hadn't gained much altitude when the student got the plane, a Swallow, into a spin.

"We stood there watching, and this Swallow went spinning down out of sight. We all started running toward the crest of the hill, expecting to see where they crashed. But before we got there, here came the plane flying back up again.

"We couldn't believe it. When Clarence landed we all ran over to see how he was. He had to be helped out of the plane because he had a sprained ankle.

"Since he hadn't crashed, we asked him how he did it. He said when the plane went into the spin, he jammed his foot on the controls, deliberately forcing it farther into the spin so reverse controls would take hold right away. When he stomped on the reverse, the plane came out with just inches to spare, but he sprained his ankle because he hit the rudder pedal so hard."

Smitty listened to this story, and turned it over in his mind. A thing like that would take a lot of guts. Someday, he thought, that will be a valuable thing to know.

There was good money in doing controlled spins in other than acrobatic flying. When the Lincoln Standard airplane was built, no one would take it up for its first test tailspin. Lincoln Aircraft Company offered fifteen hundred dollars to the pilot who would do it. A man from Oklahoma completed the test and established the reputation of a fine airplane.

As he hung around the Iola airport, Smitty was learning the

truth of what Duard had said about the *Murray Sport.* With that particular plane he could do no aerobatics because the overall design made it unstable in turns to the left.

Its motor was one of the old rotary design. In a rotary, all the cylinders whirled, creating a terrific pull, or "torque," to the left. Smitty never turned the *Murray Sport* to the left at all, for fear of losing control.

So he was limited to flying at small town celebrations and fairs, and at these all he could do was to haul passengers. If he could perform some aerobatics, he felt he could almost double his income.

One Sunday Fritz Womack took Smitty in Womack's old Jenny and deliberately put it into a tailspin. The Jennies were notoriously spin-prone. Fritz pushed her nose up, turned to the left and the next thing Merle knew they were in a spin. Smitty watched the whole process carefully; he could tell how many turns the Jenny made by watching the town come around into his view. It was just a blur, really, but he could tell it was the town. When Fritz had made one turn, enough to gain necessary speed for control, he reversed the controls. It took another two revolutions for the Jenny to come out of it. The plane started spinning at twenty-five hundred feet and when Fritz brought it under control, he had only five hundred feet on his altimeter.

With this experience behind him, Smitty felt he now knew how to control a tailspin. He thought about trying it out on the *Murray Sport,* but the pilots all advised him, "Never get that plane into a spin!" Smitty had great respect for them, but economic necessity demanded that he try.

One day at the Iola airport he took a good long look at the *Murray Sport,* sizing it up. It had a big tail and a very short nose. The motor was back close to the wings, and that was the feature the pilots said made it bad to spin. But Merle had read somewhere that if a plane had a big tail it was easy to recover from a tailspin. He drove home that night deep in thought.

The next day he got up early, drove back to Iola and rolled his *Murray Sport* out of the hangar. It was a good clear morning in late October, with a crisp invigorating feel to the air. A great day for flying.

Smitty took off, deliberately staying away from his home town of Colony, because he didn't want spectators watching if things went wrong.

He put the plane into a slow, gradual climb and kept climbing till he had gained an altitude of about eight thousand feet. The exact altitude is unknown, as the altimeter was of World War I vintage that had never been calibrated, but it was at least higher than he had ever flown the *Sport* before.

He started with a series of tight right turns. In all his flying, he had avoided left turns because of the powerful torque. He had never even dared to put the wing down on that side.

The right turns went well, so he tried a very cautious, shallow turn to the left. That worked, too, and Smitty was heartened.

He made another turn to the left, a bit steeper. The wing was down about forty-five degrees, and even though the plane felt extremely heavy on the nose, this turn, too, came out beautifully.

Merle cruised for a few minutes, feeling good over his success on the left turns. He thought he'd try a loop to see how that would work out. The plane soared up, over and around with grace and beauty.

Smitty was exhilarated, his confidence soaring. He put the *Murray Sport* into a very tight turn to the left.

About a third of the way around everything the old pilots had warned him about came true. The *Murray Sport* flopped over on its back, completely out of control, and went into a tight, vicious spin. It all happened so fast the young pilot was astounded. With powerful "G" forces pulling at him, he was terrified. He cut the master switch, hoping to stop the terrible torque to the left that held him in the tailspin, but the motor was still rotating at a high rate and there was no way to slow it down. The plane kept its dizzy, sickening descent.

Smitty reversed the controls. The plane immediately began to shudder. The shudder was so unexpected and scary that he brought the controls back to neutral. The shuddering stopped, which was a relief, but the plane continued its horrible spiral toward the spinning earth. "My eyeballs were hanging out almost to my goggles. I was petrified. But the spin continued, and it was vicious."

Not knowing what else he could do, Smitty reversed the controls again and let the plane shudder. Down he spun, wrestling the controls with all his strength to hold them against the tight, uncontrolled spiral.

Suddenly the plane gave a great heave and came out of the spin. But, it was still headed straight down, going at such a terrific speed that the wires were screaming. Smitty brought the plane out of this horrible power dive in a slow, positive recovery, to keep the wings from ripping off the airplane. He gradually leveled off, then started the motor for his return to the runway.

When Smitty landed the *Murray Sport* that clear, crisp October day, he was thoroughly convinced that this particular plane was not for aerobatics.

The End of the Murray Sport

It was shortly after the incident of the tailspin that Smitty paid a visit to an aircraft company in Lawrence, Kansas. He met and talked to the owner. Smitty had had some dealings with him in the past, and they got along well together. It was from this fellow that Duard and Henderson had bought the LeRhone engine for the *Murray Sport* and it was also the company that had marketed the learn-to-fly kits that young Merle had played with years before.

The owner had sold about ten thousand of the kits around the country, and when Smitty recounted his experience, the manager said, "Well, they should have helped you learn to fly, didn't they?" Smitty had only a caustic reply for this.

Later the manager took Smitty up for a flight in one of his planes and accidentally got the plane into a spin. He recovered it with no trouble, but Smitty couldn't help ribbing him. "I sure know where *you* learned to fly! You must have used one of your own kits."

But the plant manager and Smitty got along famously. Smitty traded in his *Murray Sport* for an OX-5 Travel Air 2000. This plane carried two passengers and the pilot. It also had an in-line engine, rather than the old rotary engine like the LeRhone. The in-line engine did away with the powerful torque associated with the rotary design and was far cleaner. The rotary engines, when they whirled, threw oil out and coated the fuselage of the airplane. Smitty had spent many hours with a putty knife, scraping oil nearly an inch thick off the fuselage of the old *Murray Sport*. It was dirty and dangerous as a fire hazard.

The new OX-5's were cleaner and more powerful. With them, Smitty felt he was in the big time. The Travel Air 2000 would recover from a spin by itself when the controls were released. But one still had to be careful with it because a few passengers would change the center of gravity. "All the old planes had to be handled like a basket of eggs," Smitty said.

During this time, hanging around the Iola airport, he was still living on the farm with his folks in Colony. One day he heard the old LeRhone engine of the *Murray Sport.* It was a sound as familiar as his own heartbeat.

He ran outside to look around. It was early in the morning, a day in late fall not long after he had sold the *Sport.* The sound of it was off to the east, and by careful listening and looking he spotted the familiar blue fuselage and orange wings of the old *Murray Sport.* It was headed south toward Oklahoma. That was the last time he saw the plane, and he didn't find out till later what happened on that flight.

The dealer had sold the *Sport* to a man from Perry, Oklahoma, and he was delivering it to its new owner. Shortly after it passed Smitty, the LeRhone engine quit — a fairly common occurrence. The pilot made a forced landing in a winter wheat field.

The landing would have been a good one, except the field the flier picked, unfortunately, had been listered.

The difference between a plowed and a listered field would not be apparent from the air to a man not familiar with farming, which this pilot was not. The farmers during the dust bowl era alternately plowed and listered their fields; plowing is smooth, listering is rough. A lister plow digs furrows, leaving the dirt turned back with ridges over the field. The wheat is planted right on the rough listered ridges, and from the air looks smooth.

The pilot landed on the rough lister ridges crosswise. The *Murray Sport* was half wood and half steel — the steel tubings connected to the wooden longerons about halfway back, just behind the pilot's cockpit. When the *Sport* bounced across a couple of the lister ridges, the plane broke in two where the wood and steel joined, and the pilot was dumped unceremoniously into the winter wheat field. The front half of the *Murray Sport* bounced on over four or five more ridges and then came to an ungraceful halt perched rakishly on its nose.

The company was understandably upset. Further inspection showed the wood was rotten where it joined the steel. Smitty learned later the company was disappointed with him for not telling them the plane was half steel and half wood. The pilot was an excellent mechanic and might have inspected the *Sport* and found the condition before the mishap. It never had occurred to young Merle that it was so important. But now, remembering the spin in the *Sport,* he got goose pimples. Suppose that wood had been ready to break while he was in the spin!

Meanwhile, Smitty was building up a repertoire of aerobatic stunts. He hired various stunt men to work with him as he moved around the country. One of the best was a young man named Carl Hall, originally hired as a parachute jumper. Carl was a fellow of steel nerve and imagination, and between them, Smitty and Carl developed some interesting and crowd-pleasing stunts, including the rope ladder. Smitty still has that ladder, and after fifty years it is one of his prize possessions.

It had hooks which snapped around the struts. It hung down under the plane and streamed out behind. Hall would climb down the ladder in a fantastic display of nerves and coordination. With the ladder streaming back, each step pulled the ladder down and he had to step upward to get hold of the next lower rung.

When he got to the bottom rung, Hall would hang by his knees while Smitty flew low over the crowd. It was a smash hit everywhere.

Hall was good at wing-walking too. It wasn't really hard, but it wasn't easy, either. The wings were full of wires to crawl between and he had to be careful where he stepped on the fabric. The stunt man usually worked in stocking feet or tennis shoes. He'd hang

Carl Hall, Smitty's parachute jumper in his first flying circus.

over the wing and wave at the crowd as they flew over, low and slow.

Another stunt man who worked with Smitty was Kidder Camp. Smitty especially remembers the time he and Kidder struck a bargain with the local Firestone Tire Company for a stunt to demonstrate the strength of their inner tube.

Kidder agreed to lower himself into the inner tube and ride around over the crowd, "trusting his very life to the strength of the Firestone inner tube!" It was the kind of stunt the barnstormers thrived on, and the crowds enjoyed. They agreed with a local Firestone dealer to do the stunt for fifteen dollars.

Since this was the first time they had attempted the stunt, Kidder didn't know one very important, seemingly minor detail: in getting down into the inner tube, an experienced stunt man would hang onto an extra rope to *lower* his weight *slowly* into the tube.

Everything started off well. Kidder Camp started down the rope to the inner tube. The crowd held its breath. Smitty made a circle and headed into the wind close to the ground, so if he had engine trouble he could land easily. Kidder, hearing the engine act up, could easily climb into the landing gear and be safe.

The plane turned into the wind and approached. The crowd held its breath.

Camp climbed down the ladder and dropped his weight into the inner tube. What he encountered was a giant sling shot.

The tube stretched to its limit, then snapped back. Kidder Camp shot out of the tube, up into the landing gear area and into the bottom of the fuselage.

Smitty, inside the plane, could not see Kidder but he felt the "thump!" Then there was dead silence. By the way the plane flew he knew there was nobody down there anymore. Did Camp fall off? What was that thump? Beads of perspiration broke out on his forehead.

He leaned over and looked out; the crowd was still standing there, looking up. If Camp had fallen off, they'd be running out onto the pasture where he had fallen. He almost certainly was still on the plane, so Smitty made a wide circle.

About halfway around, a couple of hands appeared over the leading edge of the wing, followed by a face — Kidder Camp's, scratched and bloody, as though he had tangled with a brace of wildcats. Camp had been thrown up into the landing gear and all the wires which were used to brace the airplane. His face had gone through their burry ends, but he managed to grab them and hold on. He was a bloody mess as he climbed over the leading edge of the wing and into the front cockpit.

Fritz Womack and Duard Murray, meanwhile, were working in the loft above Fritz's South Street Auto Parts store. They were building *Murray Sports,* and their infant aircraft business seemed to be coming along fine. They had built three Sports when the stock market collapse of 1929 caught them and put them out of business. After that, it was just a matter of feeding the family by any job that was available.

Barnstorming suffered too, and Merle looked around for other ways to earn money flying.

His Own Flying Circus

In the early thirties, in the depths of the depression, Merle decided to give flight instruction a whirl. He went to Winfield, Kansas, with a Waco GXE to start a flying school. "I don't know what the GXE stood for, never did find out," he said, but it was a later model of Waco 10. Winfield was a college town, and Smitty had become acquainted with a man whose son went to college there and was interested in flying.

Smitty spent the winter with Mr. and Mrs. Savoy and taught their son, Neil Savoy, to fly, but as spring came on, it became apparent that he would not be able to get enough students to make a flying school buy his beans. The Savoys were anxious, however, that Neil be given as much flight instruction as possible, so Savoy made payments on the airplane as they came due, and Smitty stayed on. Neil and Smitty formed a partnership, and decided to start their own flying circus. They were soon joined in the venture by another young fellow, Mel Hart, who didn't have much money but was an excellent mechanic.

The other thing they needed for a successful enterprise of this type was a parachute jumper. Their first performance would be held at Winfield, Kansas, on a Sunday in early spring. They lined up another pilot, Harry Krauss from Medicine Lodge, Kansas, with an OX-5 Travel Air, to do aerobatics, but they still needed a parachutist. Inquiring around the air field, they heard there was one at Anthony, Kansas.

On a rainy afternoon prior to the planned circus performance, Neil and Smitty drove to Anthony to find Carl Hall. He was working on a farm a short way out of town. Late in the evening, they found Carl in the barn, milking cows. They told him about their aerial circus, and that they needed a parachute jumper.

"I understand you've had some experience parachute jumping?" Smitty began tentatively.

"Yes," said Carl, "I made a jump last fall with an exhibition chute."

'An exhibition chute? Is that all the jumping you've done?"

"Yes."

Smitty and Neil looked at each other. Smitty said, "Well, we're still looking for a parachute jumper. We're only giving this one performance at Winfield, then we'll move on. We'll go Saturday nights to all the surrounding towns within, say, a hundred miles, and start Sunday morning with hauling passengers and putting on parachute jumps and some aerobatics, and stuff like that."

Carl went on milking. "What can I make out of that?" he asked.

Smitty said, "All I can offer is that you pass the hat to the crowd before you jump, and see what they'll pay. My guess is you'll make from ten to fifteen dollars a jump."

Carl didn't say anything. He stopped milking, got up and took the pail to the back of the barn. He hung it on a peg and walked out of the barn.

Neil and Smitty followed him, thinking he was headed for the house to get his clothes. But instead he went right to the car and asked, "Is this yours?"

"Well, yeah. But aren't you going to go get your things? Don't you have to pack or anything?"

Carl said, "This is all I've got." As they went by the house, Carl decided he'd better go in and tell the folks he was leaving.

As he got back in the car, Neil said, "I hope you make more money parachute jumping than you did here."

Carl answered, "I was only getting my room and board."

The four of them, Smitty, Neil Savoy, Mel Hart and Carl Hall, were now in business together, barnstorming. With the help of the stunt flier from Medicine Lodge, their first performance in Winfield was a great success.

For his jump, Carl used what was called an exhibition chute. It was attached to the wing struts, already open and trailing over the leading edge of the wing. Carl walked out onto the wing, stepping carefully between the wires, with the wind whipping his clothes. He sat down on the leading edge and fastened the straps of the parachute harness. He let himself down under the wing to where

Carl Hall completes one of his weekend parachute jumps for the flying circus. Before his jumps, Hall would pass his hat around for donations from spectators who were eager to see daredevil acts.

the chute was encased in a canvas bag. Pulling the slip knot loose, he was away. It was always the thrilling moment of an air show, and the crowd loved it.

It was also a dangerous stunt because so many things could go wrong. Kidder Camp, the victim of the Firestone inner tube incident, was nearly killed because two small bits of string were reversed.

An exhibition chute was normally tied to the canvas bag with something light and easily broken, like grocer's string — just enough to make the chute stream out straight before the string broke and released the chute from the bag. The bottom of the bag was tied with something stronger, like a shoestring, to support the weight of the jumper until he pulled the slip knot and released it.

One day someone tied the strings the wrong way around. When Camp's weight came to the bottom of the shrouds, where it should have broken the grocer's string and released him, it didn't.

There was Camp, held at the end of his shroud lines by a tough shoestring. He tried to climb the shrouds but it was too far. He couldn't climb the parachute silk either. He did manage to get up far enough to drop down several times and at last the shoestring broke. He was away on his jump, escaping certain tragedy. There was no way to land with him hanging there.

Herb Haley, a pilot who later flew for Smitty in Alaska, was hired just before Christmas to make a jump dressed as Santa Claus. Carrying a bag of toys, he was to land close to a group of children and begin handing out Christmas goodies.

The Bureau of Air Commerce was attempting some safety controls and had passed a rule that jumpers must have an emergency chute to back up an exhibition chute. The extra one was bulky and a nuisance, and the young daredevils of the flying circuses ignored the rule whenever possible.

On this particular flight, Herb was with a pilot named Charlie Blosser, who insisted that Herb obey the rule and carry an extra chute. Herb looked around and saw an old pack that probably had been laying on the floor of the hangar for two years. Rules also stipulated that parachutes must be freshly packed, but Herb picked up the old spare and buckled it on to satisfy Blosser.

Somewhere in the history of the exhibition chute Herb was using, the steel ring that held the shroud lines had been replaced by a Bakelite automobile steering wheel with the spokes removed. Since the jump was made in late December, the weather was extremely cold. The thermometer hovered at zero. When Herb's weight came down on that frozen Bakelite steering wheel, it shattered in a thousand pieces and Herb went hurtling through space.

Now he had only the old parachute to depend on, and he had no idea when it had last been packed or how well, or what condition the silk was in. But there was no choice. He pulled the rip-cord.

The chute blossomed out white and full above him, and he was safe. But then all sorts of things started falling around him. There were feathers, old bread and, to Herb's horror, hundreds of mice! The Santa Claus suit was rather loose-fitting around the neck and all Herb could think of was that a mouse might fall inside his shirt! He was so busy cringing and trying to close off the neck of his suit that he had no time to be thankful the chute opened. Furthermore, he forgot to direct his fall and he landed a good quarter of a mile from the waiting children. He had to hitch-hike to his eager flock, but in his distinctive red suit, it was easy to flag a ride.

The two-chute rule had not yet gone into effect that Sunday in Winfield when Smitty and his troupe put on their first aerial performance. Thereafter the little circus made visits each weekend to different small communities, putting on shows and carrying sightseers. The only money in it came from passing the hat for the parachute jumper, and from the passengers. The men

Members of Smith's flying circus pose before their plane. Back row, from left: Neil Savoy, Carl Hall, Merle Smith and Mel Hart. The men kneeling in the front were friends who helped at the airport.

augmented their income in any way they could, and at one time they were delivering fish by plane.

In 1933 the Inman Brothers Flying Circus bought Smitty's small aerial circus and hired Smitty to work with them. What they were actually after was Carl Hall, the parachute jumper. Smitty says he later read somewhere that the Inmans had bought a whole flying circus, fleas and all, to get a parachute jumper, and he figures that was probably the way it was. It illustrated the relative value, at the time, of pilots and parachutists. The Inmans had eliminated some of the competition and acquired a parachute jumper so it was a good bargain for them.

"Your Money Back If We Kill You!"

"Step right up, folks; buy an airplane ride! Don't worry about a thing — if we kill you, we'll give you your money back!"

The announcement blared forth from twin morning-glory loud-speakers mounted on the top of the big LaSalle sedan owned by the Inman Brothers Flying Circus. The crowd, already in a holiday mood, was amused by the frankness and sheer absurdity of the message.

"Buy a ride in the Ford Trimotor for fifty cents," urged the announcer. "Or a *long* ride in the Boeing Clipper for a dollar! Or a STUNT RIDE in the Stinson Detroiter for ten dollars! Step right up, folks; step right up. Don't be afraid — your money back if we kill you!"

Smitty laughs now, thinking back on it. "They'd put that right out over the air. It was an unorthodox approach, and everybody thought it was funny. It erased people's worries that we would talk about it, because in the back of their minds they were thinking 'what if I get killed?' The money-back guarantee reassured them — if we could joke about it, there must be little danger and they were encouraged to ride."

Between announcements they played snappy records to get everybody pepped up and excited. One day, Smitty recalls, they got a letter saying that they were violating all kinds of rules and regulations of the broadcast industry, and that the people who wrote the songs were entitled to a royalty on them. They ignored the whole thing, figuring that they would be moving around the country too fast for anyone to catch up with them.

The same thing happened over their use of the name Boeing Clipper. (Actually, the plane was a Boeing 80-A.) A lawyer for Pan American Airlines sent a letter saying that the company had a patent on the name Clipper, and was advertising the China Clipper to the Orient. He said the company would appreciate it very much if the Flying Circus would refrain from further use of the Clipper name.

The little troupe ignored this warning, too, for the same reason. They simply moved about the country too much to be caught. Smitty figures Pan Am probably didn't mind all that much, but it did want to be on record as having protested.

The Inman Brothers Flying Circus did, indeed, move a lot. The group would take in the smaller towns during the week, towns of two thousand, and then try to schedule the weekends in larger towns, those of five thousand or more. They stayed a week in Lincoln, Nebraska; two or three weeks in Wichita, Kansas; and Bartlesville, Oklahoma, was good for a three- or four-day stand. It wasn't profitable to stay too long. Folks got tired of it. So they kept moving about the Midwest, and Smitty received an incomparable variety of experience in flying during the three years or more with the Inman Brothers.

Before going into a town, they all met in the tiny trailer. It was crowded; all the members of the Inman Brothers Flying Circus would be there, including the two Inman wives, Leona and Margie. They gathered around the table, or wherever they could manage to write, and addressed post cards. Art Inman would take a phone book for the next town, tear the pages out and hand them around to everybody. It was his firm conviction that a hand-addressed post card interested people more and brought them out better than more impersonal ads. So, while they always put up posters and placed ads in the paper, the addressing of post cards was the most important advance advertising activity of the Inman Brothers Flying Circus. The post cards bore pictures of the planes and the members of the crew.

The cards advertised the rides and their prices, and announced that Carl Hall would make a four thousand-foot parachute jump for

A poster describes the coming of the Inman Brothers Flying Circus.

collection. Smitty did stunt flying, and was allowed to keep whatever he made hauling passengers.

Smitty learned early that the secret of a successful barnstormer was to make a lot of noise while flying over a town where they'd be playing. He developed a number of small tricks and techniques to accomplish this. The old-time planes had propellers whose pitch couldn't be changed from the cockpit, but for a fly-over, Smitty set his propeller so it would make a fearful roar. However, he couldn't carry a load that way. After noisily buzzing the town a few times, making sure everybody knew he was there, Smitty would land and reset the propeller with a wrench, a job taking about five minutes.

Members of the Inman Brothers Flying Circus are shown across the front of a post card they sent out in advance of their arrival to a town in order to drum up business. At night Smitty and his friends would meet and address the post cards from names found in the phone book. From left: Margie Inman, Leona Inman, Mel Hart, Rolley Inman, Art Inman, Carl Hall and Merle Smith.

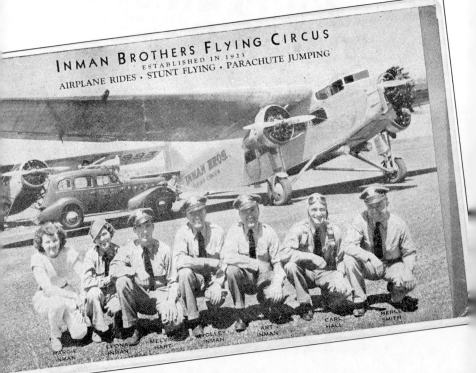

Smitty had built up an impressive repertoire of aerobatics by this time. He'd do snap rolls, slow rolls, loops, falling leafs and spins. He liked to go up and make two or three turns in a spin. When he came out of it he had a lot of speed so he could follow with a couple of loops. If he could manage it, he'd circle out of sight, come roaring in over the spectators' heads and pull up into a climb. His exhaust would be pointing at the crowd as he poured on the juice, and it made a tremendous amount of noise. The crowds ate it up.

Here again, the rugged, imaginative stunt men did their thing. There was the wing-walking, rope ladders and a host of new tricks that they conjured up.

One of the stunt men with the Inmans was LaVern Dawson, a man of iron nerve and showmanship. He would walk out on the wing, then climb onto the *upper* wing, hook his feet around the struts and grip two loops of rope tied to the wing supports. There he clung while the pilot went through loops, spins and other stunts.

Even to Smitty, the pilot, it was a heart-stopping performance. "As I went into the loop, Dawson's rear end would lift up from

Post Card

DEAR FRIEND:

The giant Boeing Clipper, America's largest tri-motor plane, and a large tri-motor Ford plane will land at the Powell-Smith field, two miles northeast of Iola, next Thursday, May 6.

You are invited to come out and see the planes and ride in them if you wish. Rides are 50c in the Ford and extra long rides are $1.00 in the Clipper.

Carl Hall will make a 4,000-foot parachute jump in the afternoon for a collection (weather permitting.)

Yours for an airplane ride,
—ART INMAN.

Sec. 562 P. L. &
U. S. POSTAG
PAID
Permit No. 1
IOLA, KANSA

Arbuckle
Garage

IOLA, KANSAS

where he sat on the wing and it looked like he'd fly right off. After that, I couldn't see what he was doing because I was too busy flying, but on the other half of the loop he'd be plastered down tight to the wing because of the centrifugal force.

"Nowadays these same stunts are done with steel cables and harnesses that take all the risk out, but Dawson did it just hanging on to two coils of rope and with his feet hooked around the struts. Just by brute strength. He was really tremendous."

The old biplanes were popular for such flying because the extra wing gave them a lot of lift for getting off the small fields that were so prevalent then. But during his stint with the Inmans, Smitty did some flying with the Ford Trimotor, and found it a fine airplane. He yearned for some stunt flying in it. He always took the parachute jumper up in the Ford Trimotor, with the side doors off so he could make his jumps.

One day Smitty told Carl he was going to go up higher, after Carl jumped, and try a few loops. Carl said it was a great idea. When Carl jumped, Smitty climbed another thousand feet and started a loop. He stalled at the top. In this upside down position the gas drained away from the carburetors, two of the three engines quit, and the third one popped sluggishly.

He was hanging by his safety belt, and things started flying out the open side door. Even the back of his seat came loose and went out the window, which Smitty kept open on a hot day.

At last the nose of the Ford came down. The plane picked up speed, allowing Smitty to make a split-S recovery and restart the motors. Those few agony-filled moments seemed like an unhappy lifetime. Not having a seat back didn't help much either. From the ground, it was a great show.

Smitty was paid a stipend for the aerobatics, plus whatever he could get flying passengers afterward. The Inmans usually timed the aerial performance for late afternoon, after the farmers had finished their chores. Then, after the stunts and the parachute jump, darkness began to fall and they'd go into the business of night flying of passengers.

Night flying was relatively new and all the rage. The customers got a whole new view of their world. They could see the lights of their town, of their farm, and the countryside for miles around.

The fliers developed some rudimentary techniques for this type of flying. They marked the field with four kerosene lanterns. The first lanterns showed where it was clear to set down and the last were the end of the field.

The first summer with the Inmans, Smitty flew his own Travel Air, but about the middle of the season he cracked it up, and that put him out for the rest of the season. The next year the Inmans hired him back to fly their Stinson. But the job was for only eight or nine months of the year. Times were hard, and it was tough to make ends meet during the winter layoffs, though the Inmans tried to spread what little overhaul work there was between the crew members. One winter Smitty worked at the Stearman factory in Wichita, which had a government contract to build eighty planes for the Brazilian government.

Smitty won a number of flying prizes during those years — for making a perfect dead stick landing on the mark, and first prize in "balloon busting." In balloon busting, the flier is in the air when a balloon filled with helium is released. It rises swiftly and is very elusive. When it reaches a designated altitude, the pilot tries to fly into it to burst it. Unless it is hit perfectly, the balloon will slither through the propeller or bounce off. Smitty managed to break his balloon in nineteen seconds, just two seconds short of the record. It was a great spectator sport.

Another enviable mark was set in 1936 when he flew more than twenty-six thousand passengers for the flying circus.

Yet he could see the shortcomings of the work, and was fully aware of the hazards involved. He began to look around for other flying jobs, something more permanent than the flying circus, but as he inquired around he found there was just nothing at all for pilots.

Early in his career with the Inmans, Smitty had met Merritt D. Kirkpatrick at the Swallow Aircraft Company in Wichita. It was years before Smitty knew Kirkpatrick's first name because he was always called "Kirk," or more formally, M.D. Kirkpatrick. Kirk had been ferrying supplies and passengers to Alaska during the winters, and was full of stories about the legendary Alaska bush pilots who, it seemed, always got through and flew in the toughest kind of weather. Smitty was still young enough to be highly impressionable and he listened goggle-eyed to these stories, in the same way he had listened to radio accounts about World War I pilots.

"You ought to go to Alaska," Kirk told him, but Alaska seemed too far away and too exotic to be seriously considered. Smitty continued with the circus.

During the spring of 1937 it went to Wichita and stayed there a week barnstorming. Smitty was flying the Ford that season. While in Wichita he made a number of contacts regarding jobs as a pilot, and he kept in touch with his contacts for several months, but nothing developed.

One of his Wichita friends was Irl Beech. Irl mentioned a friend of his at Cordova, Alaska, who had a small operation there. Irl suggested that if Smitty wanted to go to Alaska, there might be an opening there.

Alaska again. And the friend was none other than M.D. Kirkpatrick. Kirk had gone to Cordova in 1934 and started up Cordova Air Service. He was offering Smitty a chance to become one of those legendary Alaska bush pilots.

But Smitty still felt Alaska was too much of a gamble to consider. For one thing, he didn't have enough money to make the trip up there, and it didn't seem he would ever make enough. But he took the name and address and the flying circus moved on.

In July, right after the Fourth, the Inman Circus was at Wheatland, Wyoming. It was an extremely hot day, and the air was poor for flying. Adding to the difficulty was the high altitude at Wheatland. The Ford was powered by J-5 nonsupercharged engines, and Smitty was having a great deal of trouble getting airborne. He had to fly all the time on full throttle. Art Inman's Boeing had more power and lifting surface than the Ford, but Art, too, was experiencing lift trouble. They talked it over, and Art suggested that Smitty cut his payload from twelve to ten passengers, which he did. They were flying off a big plateau and were surrounded by wide, deep canyons.

As the day wore on, it seemed to get hotter and the flying conditions worse. Smitty hoped that with darkness, things would cool off, but his hopes were in vain. The heat stayed on, and if anything, it was hotter.

The boys came out with their kerosene lanterns, and the night flying began. As Smitty made his runs, he used the lights of a ranch house off across the canyon to tell him when to make his turn to the field. It made a definite marker for him to fly by.

Things went fine in the early part of the evening, but about eleven o'clock, the rancher went to bed. When Smitty made his next turn, there was no light there to mark his turn.

It was an extremely dark night, but Smitty had been flying long enough to anticipate something like this. He had checked his wrist watch for the time used in making the turn. Now he allowed forty-five seconds after leaving his last marker, and went into the turn.

He landed fine. It was an uncomfortable feeling, though, to

think what might have happened if he hadn't been timing his turns.

The group went back to town about midnight, after the crowd thinned out and there were no more riders. Smitty sat up quite late, thinking long and hard. He felt he was not long for this world if he kept up the sort of thing he had had to do that day. Remembering the name and address in his wallet, he wrote to Kirkpatrick in Alaska. Another letter went to Irl Beech in Wichita, telling him that he had applied for the job in Cordova and asking for a letter of recommendation.

All the mail went to Alaska by sea in those days, so the letter Smitty wrote to Kirk and the letter of recommendation Irl Beech wrote traveled north on the same ship.

The flying circus, meanwhile, moved to Lusk, Wyoming, and flew some of the small towns around there. They turned east and down through Scott's Bluff, Nebraska, worked their way through the rich, irrigated valley where business was always good, and wound up two or three weeks later in York, Nebraska.

One Saturday in York, as Smitty sat in the shade of the hangar, a telegram was delivered to him from Cordova. It was a job offer, twelve months a year employment at $175 a month.

People who came to see the flying circus often hung around, visiting the pilots before and after performances. Among the visitors the day Smitty got the telegram was Bertha Oglesby. Bertha was a telephone operator, and she went to the office to place a long distance call for Smitty. He wanted Cordova on the line. She found there was no long distance telephone in Cordova; the farthest she could get the call was to Juneau, still about four hundred miles from Cordova.

The next fastest communication was a telegram, which Smitty sent immediately, saying he was interested in the job but had no money to get to Alaska. The next day he got a wire from Kirk, telling him there was a ship ticket for him in Seattle.

Smitty gave notice to Art Inman and started preparations to go north. He didn't like to leave the Inmans; he felt they had given him a chance to develop his flying and had been good friends, too. But he knew they would have little trouble replacing him. There were a number of good pilots around who were available. One was Jack Jefford, a pilot Smitty had come to know quite well.

Jefford was flying at Hastings, Nebraska, and Smitty went to see him. Jefford had been flying all afternoon, diving on the crowds, pulling up, and generally creating enough excitement so that people would run over and buy a ride with him in his plane. It was common practice, but by then the Bureau of Air Commerce was trying to exercise a little control over pilots and their practices. When Smitty arrived at the hangar he found Jefford talking to a Bureau Inspector named Montay. Smitty didn't want to talk to Mr. Montay either, so he left without saying goodbye.

A few months later, in Alaska, Jack Jefford showed up piloting a Vega that belonged to Hans Mirrow of Nome. Smitty took up where he had left off in Hastings.

"What did old Montay want to see you about?" Smitty asked.

Jack laughed. "Oh, he just wanted to raise hell about my flying. Accused me of diving down on the crowd."

Smitty grinned. It was just part of the life of a barnstormer, but now they both had put those days behind them.

FIRST YEARS IN ALASKA

North to Alaska

The telegram from Kirk had requested Smitty to get a flight rating for the Stearman C3B biplane before coming north. It seemed a simple enough rating, but after he arrived in Alaska, he found that there was only one Bureau of Air Commerce inspector in the entire territory and ratings of any kind were very difficult to arrange.

Smitty had his ticket from Seattle to Cordova, but apparently it hadn't occurred to Kirk that Smitty might not have enough money to get to Seattle. Smitty began his trip from York, Nebraska, by hitch-hiking. From Kansas City he was able to buy a bus ticket to Wichita, then made his way on to Chanute, Kansas.

There he contacted Dr. Johnson, a Bureau of Air Commerce examiner, who examined Smitty for his pilot's physical. Smitty had great affection and respect for Dr. Johnson, and it must have been returned in kind, for Smitty was able to stall payment for the doctor's fee. When he told Johnson that he needed money to go to Alaska, the physician gave him a personal check for forty dollars.

Smitty's Union Pacific ticket cost thirty-four dollars, coach. He sat up, sleeping in his seat. Smitty thoroughly enjoyed the trip. A new friend he made on the way was an old Alaskan sourdough from McGrath named Buckskin Bill.

When Buckskin found that the young pilot was going to Alaska and was apparently on short rations, Bill took him under his wing and from then on Smitty didn't go hungry. When they reached Seattle, Smitty had planned on walking from the King Street Station to the Alaska Steamship Company pier, but Buckskin wouldn't hear of it. He hailed a cab and the two of them rode to the dock together.

The steamship ticket included meals, so Smitty's small cache of money was not needed aboard the ship. He looked his little hoard over and saw ten dollars and a bit of change, which had to last him till payday in Cordova. He longed for a cigarette, but decided against it.

Ship travel to Alaska was extremely pleasant. It was a leisurely six-day voyage to Cordova on the old *Yukon*, the most popular vessel in the Alaska Steamship Company fleet.

As Smitty stood on the deck of the *Yukon*, watching the lights of the town of Cordova approach, he was entering a brand new world of flying. Aviation in Alaska was new, as it was in the rest of the country, but in Alaska it had a special place. Roads were almost nonexistent. Distances between towns and even isolated cabins were many times greater than on the "Outside," as people called the states. The territory needed transportation desperately. Dog team travel was grueling, slow, uncertain and limited to mid-winter. There were two major railroads, the Alaska Railroad north from Anchorage, and the Copper River & Northwestern Railway from Cordova to the Kennecott Copper Company mines through Chitina, McCarthy and Kennicott.*

The pilots occupied a special esteem in Alaska. They brought mail and groceries to the winter-bound miners in their lonely cabins, supplies to the isolated gold and copper mines, mail to tiny villages. Aviation names were already becoming famous — the bush pilots of Alaska such as Carl Ben Eielson, who had brought the first plane north to Fairbanks and imbued the people of that interior city with the flying spirit. It was Eielson who flew the first air mail in Alaska. He crashed and died while on a fur-ferrying flight to Siberia.

There were the brothers Wien — Noel, Fritz, Sigurd and Ralph, who had an air service in the gold country near Nome. There was a brash young pilot, Bob Reeve, flying out of Valdez and making daring landings on glaciers to supply isolated mines. There was "Thrill 'em, spill 'em, never kill 'em Gillam" — Harold Gillam, the dark-browed, moody pilot who could fly anywhere, any time.

There were other aviation names which have now become almost legendary: Hans Mirrow and Murrel W. "Sass" Sasseen, to name a couple, besides a number who were to become fast friends and archrivals of Merle as the years went by — Ray Petersen, Jack Peck, Art Woodley and others.

When Merle arrived in Cordova, the first flight into that area was only eight years past. It was in May of 1929 that Clayton Scott landed on Eyak Lake near Cordova with a Gorst Air Transport Loening Amphibian plane, to the wild sounding of whistles, bells and cheers from a waiting crowd. The flight, billed as the "Conquest of the Gulf of Alaska," originated in Juneau and took four hours and thirty-six minutes, after waiting a week for weather.

In 1931, two years after that first landing in Cordova, Harold Gillam began flying out of Cordova in a Swallow. In 1934

---

*The apparent discrepancy in spelling is because the town of Kennicott was named after Robert Kennicott, an early Alaska explorer; the company, Kennecott Copper Company, was spelled differently due to a spelling error in applying for official papers for the corporation. The two remain spelled differently to this day.

M.D. Kirkpatrick established Cordova Air Service and was attempting to bring a semblance of scheduled flight to the stormy, glacier-laced country around Alaska's southern coast. It was a country of drifting fog, blinding snow squalls, and incredibly swift weather changes; a place where pilots flew through narrow mountain passes that could sock in solid within minutes. There were no navigation aids, and the radio communications were extremely sketchy. Phone service was available along the Copper River Railroad line at the section houses, but it was not what you would call reliable.

Captain Austin E. Lathrop, Alaska's only resident millionaire at the time, a businessman who consistently plowed his money back into Alaska, had built the hangars at Cordova's Eyak Field and had leased them to Kirkpatrick with an option to buy at a later date. "Cap" Lathrop was well known as a promoter, but his name is never cited as an early supporter of aviation. However, he obviously was, because the Cordova hangars were among the very first in Alaska, and must have been a rather risky venture.

When Smitty arrived in Cordova he spotted a tall, lanky fellow with a pencil-line mustache standing on the dock, peering anxiously at the passengers on the ship. Smitty had little trouble recognizing Kirk Kirkpatrick, and the two greeted each other like long lost buddies.

Kirk took Smitty's bag and threw it in the back of an old battered pickup truck. Then they were off down the dirt road toward town, bumping through chuckholes and raising a cloud of dust.

"Boy, am I glad to see you!," said Kirk. "I've got a flight for you right now. Did you get that rating I asked you to?"

Smitty assured him that he had the rating.

A two-block drive took them clear through the business district of Cordova. Mountains rose abruptly on all sides, thickly forested and covered with dense underbrush, almost like a jungle. It was not at all what Smitty had expected of Alaska.

They turned up a side road that led to Eyak Lake. Like a jewel in a magnificent setting, the lake shimmered green in the summer sun, mirroring the verdant mountains. Along the edge, chiseled out of the base of the peak, lay the Eyak Lake airstrip. Hangars hugged the steep mountain slope, and the gravel runway was built out into the water.

The old truck rattled to a stop in front of a hangar. A sign tacked to a wooden door proclaimed "Office."

Smith Field

Kirk offered Smitty a cup of coffee and got down to business. Smitty was to fly to McCarthy, about 150 miles north on the Copper River, in an open cockpit Stearman C3B biplane.

"You can't miss McCarthy," Kirk assured him. "Just follow the railroad tracks." After a briefing over the maps, Smitty left for his first flight in Alaska.

He got to McCarthy without incident, and started back down the Copper River valley, mountains on either side, following the sandy, twisting river course, when he spotted a thick bank of fog ahead.

The fog came within minutes, rolling up the river valley from the sea. This was something new to the young pilot. It was common along the Alaska coast, but rare in the Midwest.

Mindful of the stories of Alaska bush pilots who always finished their flights and never turned back, Smitty flew right into the fog bank, staying low over the railroad tracks.

He figured if he stayed with them, he could follow the tracks and get through to Cordova. He entered the fog bank at about Mile 50 (as measured by the railroad from Cordova).

The water was on his right as he progressed toward Mile 39, and the fog got progressively thicker and lower. The river basin was several miles wide, so Smitty felt he had a margin of freedom for any maneuver he might need in following the rails. But after six or seven more miles, it was just too thick. Common sense took over, and he made a 180 degree turn back up the river out of the fog.

As he flew back, he kept thinking of the stories he had heard, that real Alaska bush pilots always got through.

"There was something about this fog that I didn't understand," he said. "Alaska bush pilots apparently could fly in that kind of fog. I'd flown in fog in the Midwest in the wintertime, but this was different. Still, I'd heard that Alaska bush pilots never failed, so I told myself I was being chicken. I turned around toward Cordova and started following the railroad tracks again.

"I went another mile or two farther than I did the first time, then better judgment told me I should turn back."

At Mile 63 the little plane burst from the white shroud into brilliant sunshine. Merle just couldn't understand such peculiar weather conditions. He climbed the Stearman to get above the cloud layer and take a look around, but as far as the eye could see, the white blanket rose higher and higher.

Still, he thought, as long as he could see how it lay, he ought to be able to get through it.

For the third time he turned toward Cordova and entered the thick white mist.

He flew on through the murk, following the railroad tracks so low he almost brushed the treetops. He flashed over a section camp at Mile 39. The men had just finished eating and were out in front of the section house when the little plane darted past. Smitty had a glimpse of surprised faces turned upward as he disappeared into the fog. He lost the railroad, found it again and then, almost out of fuel, had to look for a landing place.

The Copper River in this area has a wide basin to follow, but is surrounded by precipitous mountains, with glaciers crawling down their flanks. The river is a shallow, swift torrent with shifting sand bars and grassy places along its edges. In midstream sand bars of dubious duration exist. Along the riverbanks ran the Copper River & Northwestern Railway, with occasional trackwalkers' cabins and section houses. Smitty spotted a section house at Mile 78, and picked out a place to land. It was covered with high grass, the kind of place he commonly landed on in Kansas.

What Smitty didn't know was that in Alaska you never land on high grass and brush land — it's all swamp and tundra. He brought his plane down and rolled to a nice even landing. By pure chance he had picked the only good, solid spot around. This particular swampy area had a strip about eight hundred feet long and twenty-five feet wide through it that would support a landing. Twenty feet on either side and he'd have had a nasty crash.

Oblivious to his good fortune and still convinced that he was a failure as a bush pilot, Smitty went over to the section house and was taken in, fed and housed overnight. Had he been an experienced bush pilot, he would have landed on a sand bar in the middle of the river and probably would have spent a miserable night with the plane. Ignorance sometimes pays off.

The railroad section houses were connected by a single telephone line of doubtful integrity, but it offered the only communication from that part of the country. Late that night Smitty got through to F.A. Hansen, who was with the railroad and a major stockholder in Cordova Air Service.

Hansen had been on the phone for three hours, frantically calling the railroad section houses all the way from Chitina to Cordova for any news of the missing pilot. Everyone in Cordova had written him off as a casualty on his first flight.

Merle Smith soon after his arrival to Alaska. (Portrait by Marvin Roark, courtesy of Merle Smith)

Over the phone Smitty recounted his story in great detail — leaving out the feelings of failure, of course. He told Hansen where he was and what had happened.

"I'm low on gas," Smitty explained, "but I'll fly on into Cordova in the morning if the fog lifts."

"Okay," said F.A., "don't take any chances. I'll see you later."

Then Smitty turned in, still assailed by doubts about his own ability, and tortured by a sense of failure. The future seemed bleak indeed, and he tossed and turned a long time before falling into a troubled sleep.

Next morning, finding the sun shining brightly along the green banks of the river, Smitty flew on to town where he was eagerly questioned about his experiences. When they heard about the place where he landed, they were all astounded. Harold Gillam, flying over the marshy meadow later (he could see the wheel marks where the plane had landed), said he was absolutely amazed at Smitty's luck. They dubbed it Smith Field. Smitty used it a number of times afterward, but from then on, except for Smith Field, Smitty always made his forced landings on hardpacked sand bars in the river.

As Smitty piled up experience flying the Copper River over the next few months, he found that the lingering sense of self-doubt he had felt that day stayed with him for a long time. Even after he became convinced that Alaska bush pilots were not the epitome of success — they frequently could not, after all, get through the weather — he still remained troubled by a feeling of inadequacy. He had confidence in his flying, but he never seemed able to shake that lingering doubt until, later that year, he had a long talk with Harold Gillam.

Gillam's name was legendary. He was the man who always got through, according to the stories. Indeed, he was a skilled, steel-nerved pilot with an incredible record. Subconsciously, Smitty had been pitting himself against both the record and the legend of "Thrill 'em, Spill 'em, Never Kill 'em Gillam." It was an impossible thing to do.

Smitty, in going over his anxieties, had given a lot of thought to the "point of no return," which was a big thing to pilots in those days. It meant, simply, that at a certain point in a flight, if the weather was bad or marginal, it was better to turn and go back because after that point there wouldn't be enough gas either to get through or go home.

The point of no return was what Smitty had passed that day on the Copper River when he couldn't get back to McCarthy.

Smitty was telling Gillam about his first flight. He asked the older pilot what he thought about the point of no return.

Gillam swore. "That goddam point of no return has killed more good pilots than anything that I know. I just forget it. If you get beyond the point of no return, you have to try harder, and usually you make it to where you were going."

Smitty was impressed with this advice, and tried to follow it after that. As long as he could still see, he just kept flying, and he found that he generally made it through — if not to the exact place he was headed, at least to someplace near by. He found he was more relaxed when he forgot about the point of no return, and his confidence began to build again.

Smitty had arrived in Alaska with only a few dollars in his pocket. He made arrangements to pay his hotel bill out of September's paycheck, and looked around for ways to stretch his food rations. What he didn't know was that everyone charged his food at the Model Cafe, and no one gave it a second thought. Merle's Kansas upbringing didn't include charging anything. That was unheard of.

But he soon found ways to cope. One of his main stops was at McCarthy, where Cordova Air Service maintained a cabin for its pilots. The reasoning was that the company didn't want to pay any hotel bills for pilots. The cabin had a good stove and everything needed for cooking. In the corner was a barrel buried in the ground, where butter and meat could be stored. Since the barrel was into the permafrost, it made a fine refrigerator. Best of all, groceries could be charged to Cordova Air Service.

Smitty was always happy when he made a stop at McCarthy, and he tried to get such trips as often as possible. At the cabin, he

Cordova Air Service provided this cabin in McCarthy in order to avoid the cost of boarding its pilots in town. While at the cabin, Smith would store up on free food. Pictured are two of Smith's friends.

would eat as much as he could, sometimes to the point of discomfort, hoping to make the meal last longer. Often he would swipe a can of beans or other food and bring it to Cordova, where he would smuggle it into his hotel room. He was careful not to leave the empty cans laying about, so no one would know how meager his money supply was.

Eventually August slipped by, a month of flying, for the most part, to McCarthy and the Bremner Mine. These two points formed the backbone of Cordova Air Service's business. With the end of the month, Smitty got his first real paycheck and began to put money aside. As soon as he had enough ahead, he planned to send for Bertha Oglesby, back in York, Nebraska.

August was an eventful month for Smitty. It gave him a wealth of new experiences and added two other things of lasting significance. One was his beaver hat. The other became a more lasting trademark, one which he didn't appreciate until many years had passed — his nickname "Mudhole."

"Mudhole" and the Beaver Hat

Flying to the Bremner Mine was all in a day's work for Smitty. Many of the directors of Cordova Air Service were heavy investors in the Bremner Mining Company, and they were keen that the mine should be well serviced during the summer months when the cleanup was coming in. It also made for better relations with the miners, who liked to get their mail and newspapers by air.

The old Stearman could haul six hundred pounds of freight. No horses were kept at the mines, so the airstrip was built as close as possible to the mine buildings. At the Bremner Mine, it was on spongelike tundra a few hundred yards north of the main building and the cook shack.

On each side of this level bit of soggy earth they dug ditches for what drainage could be obtained. The ditches were about 50 feet apart. In between, in a strip down the middle about 20 feet wide and 250 to 300 feet long, they laid large flat shale type rocks, some as big as a table top. They were all pushed together as closely as they could be made to fit.

The old Stearman carried a tail skid instead of a tail wheel, and on landing often uprooted a rock in the middle of the field.

On a day of heavy rain squalls, Smitty was anxious to get off the ground before the weather closed in. He often had been warned by Kirk to walk back over the field to see that there were no rocks misplaced, but Smitty thought he had kept the tail up long enough on landing and had not dislodged any stones. He climbed in the Stearman and taxied out for takeoff.

Smitty had guessed wrong about the tail skid. It had caught a large stone and slid it up on top of another, leaving a big muddy hole.

As the Stearman gathered speed down the runway, the left wheel dropped into the hole and sank in the mud. The plane slewed off the rocky center strip and stood on its nose. Since the propeller was turning at about eighteen hundred revolutions per minute, it acted like a big auger, digging the entire nose into the soft spongy ground.

Smitty could see the miners running in his direction.

"Are you okay?" they asked as they came up to the plane.

"Sure," growled Smitty, clawing at his safety belt. "Help me out of here."

He surveyed the mess and was sure he had ruined the motor, the prop, the whole works.

"They're bringing up the tractor," a miner said. "Maybe we can tow it out of here."

By taking it nice and easy, the tractor managed to pull the nose out of the mud.

When Smitty examined it closely, he was astonished to find that the prop hadn't been bent at all! There was an awful gob of mud, though, around it and the motor.

Now that the incident was over and no one was hurt, the miners began to crack jokes about it. Smitty smiled gamely at the rough sourdough humor, but he really wasn't amused. There was no water at the mine to spare for the cleanup job, so he was going to have to scrape all the mud off by hand. The only tool he could find was a screwdriver. It looked like an all-night job.

The tractor pulled the plane to one end of the field and Smitty began scraping. He had to be very careful to remove all the mud from around the louvers of each cylinder, because the engine was air-cooled. He sat on a stepladder while he worked at the tedious chore.

There was no radio in the plane, but Kirk had installed a one-tube transmitter at the mine so the directors could keep in touch each day. Nine o'clock was the scheduled time for radio contact with Cordova. Lew Cochran was the radio operator. As soon as Lew had Kirk on the radio, he handed the mike to Smitty.

Kirk had been worried for hours about his missing pilot. Smitty explained that he had been stuck in a blasted mudhole. As soon as the night's frost had frozen the ground, he could take off, probably about 4 A.M. Kirk said okay, but to be sure to check everything carefully before trying it.

Smitty spent the remainder of the night scraping mud. Early in the morning, with the ground frozen, Smitty took off from the Bremner Mine and returned to Cordova without further incident.

Sooner or later in Alaska, everyone acquired a nickname. Bob Reeve was flying out of Valdez and making a name for himself as the "Glacier Pilot" for his landings on glaciers near remote mountain-top mines.

The bush grapevine had spread the story of Smitty's misadventure and the next time Reeve saw Smitty, he greeted him as "Mudhole Smith." To Smitty's chagrin, the name stuck. It was years before he really appreciated the jaunty good humor in the sourdough nickname.

Not all flights were so mundane as flying freight to the mines. One of Smitty's earliest trips was to bring Cap Lathrop to Cordova for a director's meeting.

Smitty had often heard of Alaska's first and only millionaire. Captain Austin E. Lathrop. Lathrop was interested in buildings, theaters and radio stations throughout Alaska as well as financing the hangars at Eyak Field. He had five shares of Cordova Air Service stock, possibly the only stock he ever held. He owned other businesses outright.

As a shareholder in Cordova Air Service, he traveled quite a distance to attend meetings of the board of directors. Usually, he used surface transportation, but this year he decided to fly from Fairbanks for the meeting in Cordova.

Mudhole was chosen as the pilot, something of an honor for an Alaska fledgling. Smitty had never seen a real live millionaire up close, and he was quite excited about it.

A yellow Stinson Reliant was used for the flight. It was a beautiful aircraft, with good upholstery and comfortable seats. The crews set about polishing it inside and out till it shone. "Probably the cleanest any airplane ever was for years before and years after," declared Mudhole.

Smitty flew to Fairbanks and picked up Alaska's most prominent personage. Cap Lathrop met him at Weeks Field, and as they gassed the plane, Cap was as full of questions as a schoolboy. Smitty was surprised and pleased with Cap's style. He was just like anyone else, maybe even more concerned about his friends than most. He had friends all over the territory, and he kept track of them by asking after them whenever he had a chance. He eagerly questioned Smitty about acquaintances in McCarthy, Chitina, Kennicott and Cordova.

They took off in beautiful weather for Cordova. Although the plane carried plenty of gas, Smitty decided on a hunch to stop in Chitina and top off the tank.

Once more, Cap was full of questions. "Why did we stop here?" he asked.

"I just want to be sure we have enough gas," Smitty replied.

"The weather's all right, isn't it?"

Once again, Smitty reassured him. "Yes. My last report was that it was good."

Smitty explained that it was easier and safer to keep plenty of gas on board than to take any chances.

Lathrop mentioned Northwest Airlines' new Martin 202's. "Pretty good plane," he observed. "Fast. Really fast. They can pass up everything but a filling station."

Smitty grinned. He was beginning to get the picture: when Cap Lathrop went somewhere, he liked to keep going. He didn't like having to stop for things like extra gas. He was impatient of such delays, but during the flight from Chitina, it was Lathrop himself who asked for a gas-consuming detour around a large but localized rain shower. Mudhole didn't mind. It added some 10 minutes or so to the flight but Smitty was comfortable in the knowledge that he had plenty of fuel.

All the Cordova people who were in business with Cap were at Eyak Field to meet them. Smitty was amazed at how many there were. In the years to come, he also enjoyed a long friendship with Cap Lathrop.

Another prominent local person Smitty carried as a passenger was "Doc" Chase, Cordova's perennial mayor who held that elected position for some thirty years.

Kirk hoped to build up business with Anchorage, and it was important that his new pilot learn the route. Since Kirk himself couldn't go along on the first flight, he looked around for someone else to guide Smitty.

Doc Chase seemed the logical choice. He was an avid sportsman, a guide and the author of several books about hunting in

Alaska. He held Guide's License No. 1 from the Fish & Wildlife Service, and was allowed to keep it after he grew too old to go out hunting. His knowledge of the country was without question. He also was a stockholder in Cordova Air Service.

They took off in a Bellanca on a beautiful sunny day. They crossed the waters of Prince William Sound, with its forested islands, fjords, glaciers and the snowclad Chugach Mountains in the distance ahead. The route through the mountains was Portage Pass and it was Doc Chase's job to identify Passage Canal, the fjord leading to the pass.

Even though he knew every inch of the country from the ground, Doc found it completely different from the air. Try as he would, he couldn't show Smitty which of the many deep fjords was the right one.

"If I was in a boat, I could tell you," he insisted. Smitty knew this was so, but it was no help to him now. The other passengers were beginning to fidget in their seats.

If he couldn't get through the mountains, he would have to go over them. It was a clear day, so he climbed to twelve thousand feet. From there he could see Turnagain Arm and follow it to Anchorage with no trouble. The lesson he learned was that a pilot should never allow anyone but another pilot to guide him.

Doc Chase was also a historian and miner. On the way back he showed Smitty the location of all the mines on the islands and nearby mainland, and the knowledge was of great value to Mudhole in subsequent years.

Smitty flew many flights to Anchorage after that. On one trip he acquired a beaver hat. He never really appreciated the "Mudhole" nickname until many years had passed, but from the very first he liked being associated with that hat.

Two women from Nabesna ran afoul of the law and were given until nightfall to get out of Cordova. They had worked the town long enough to have money, so they went to Cordova Air Service and told Kirk they wanted to charter a plane to Anchorage. Kirk, being a married man and a prudent one, assigned the job of flying them to Mudhole — who was unmarried.

The two women really enjoyed the flight. They regaled Smitty with tales of their misadventures. One had heard of Smitty's new nickname and howling with laughter, recounted the story to the other so they both could kid the pilot about it.

When they got to Anchorage, one woman decided to give Mudhole a gift. She had in her suitcase a brand new man's fur hat, a gift from a Nabesna miner who had fallen in love with her. She hadn't really wanted the hat in the first place, she dug it out and placed it on Smitty's head.

It was a perfect fit. It was of beaver fur, with earflaps that tied over the top or could be let down when the wind was cold in the Stearman's open cockpit. Smitty liked the hat right away, and wore it so often it became almost as much of a trademark as "Mudhole." Its origin only added to its general appeal.

Walking Out

Although Cordova Air Service was only three years old, already there was a brisk business with Southeastern Alaska. The Civil Aeronautics Board wasn't yet in the picture and nearly all flying was done by charter.

Smitty made a number of the flights, long grueling trips with frequent refueling stops. A typical flight started at eight o'clock in the morning if possible. More often, it was nine o'clock before the weather report came through by Alaska Communications System wire, and then it was ten o'clock before all the passengers could be rounded up and put on board. With the two hour difference in time, it was already noon in Juneau before he could get away from Cordova.

There were no landing fields. The trip was made in a Bellanca on floats, a plane Smitty liked although it had one grave shortcoming. It had to be flown as if it had no stick control — no aileron. The stick was so close to the side of the plane that by the time he put his foot on the pedal, with his knee in the way, there was only about an inch leeway for moving the stick. If the wing went down, it was extremely hard to get it back up, so Smitty flew it as though it had no stick control at all. It wasn't too bad, except in rough weather. With the wind kicking the plane around, it would yaw back and forth and make all the passengers sick.

Still, a Bellanca performed well on floats, and packed a big load of freight in addition to the passengers, so Smitty insists it was a good airplane.

One of two Bellancas of the Cordova Air Service had a 112-gallon gas tank, the other held only 80 gallons. Yakutat, halfway across the Gulf of Alaska, was the first refueling stop. To get there took about two hours and forty minutes, with favorable flight conditions.

At Yakutat he would land and taxi up to the cannery dock. There were no fueling facilities — he had to carry the gas to the dock in five-gallon cans, two at a time, and lower them on a rope. He climbed down the ladder to the float and tied one of the cans to it, so it wouldn't tip over while he poured the other into the tank through a funnel. Since the plane took at least fifty gallons, the better part of an hour and a half was spent refueling.

Then he was off to Juneau, hoping not to encounter fog at Cape Spencer. With the eighty-gallon Bellanca, it was really a "short gas" situation if he had to turn back and seek shelter in one of the glacier bays along the coast such as Lituya.

Under the best of conditions, the last half of the flight to Juneau took another two hours and forty minutes, so it was better than seven hours from Cordova to Juneau under good flying conditions. In Juneau he had to gas up again before going on to whichever Southeastern city was his final destination: Wrangell, Petersburg, Ketchikan, Hoonah and occasionally Sitka. The Southeast run averaged two or three trips a week.

Kirk was flying it with four or five passengers, including his wife Dean, when they encountered fog at Icy Bay. Kirk got a little too close to the mountains and his wing caught in the trees. The small plane went down, spilling them into the timber. No one was hurt, but the nearest radio station was at Cape Yakataga, about fifty miles away. There was little chance for rescue unless they walked the whole way, so they started out.

The beach along the northern rim of the Gulf of Alaska slopes down steeply to the water's edge, and they walked for three days along this sideways slope. Dean and Kirk both declared that it was a horrible experience — they felt as if one leg was shorter than the other for a long time afterward.

After that Kirk began to lose interest in Southeastern flights and business declined in that direction. He continued to fly the Cape Yakataga and Yakutat mail runs under subcontract to Harold Gillam, who had postal contracts to these points on the Gulf of Alaska.

During the really cold part of the winter of 1937-38, Smitty flew a charter for a young game warden, Clarence Rhode. He later became very well known, and a national wildlife refuge in Alaska was named for him.

Rhode had been in Alaska only a few months. The Fish & Wildlife Service was having trouble with smugglers of wolf fur. Trappers brought furs across the border from Canada, where there was no bounty, to sell them in the U.S. and collect the bounty. It was a fairly widespread and lucrative practice, according to Fish & Wildlife Service estimates. Clarence hired Cordova Air Service to fly him on a patrol along the Canadian border.

It was a bitterly cold day in January when the two men set out from McCarthy. They flew first over Horsefeld Lake and then north parallel to the border. They planned to fly as far as Fortymile, watching for sled and toboggan trails in the snow, and spend the night in Dawson City.

North of Horsefeld Lake, Mudhole noticed the number one cylinder on the plane's engine was weaving back and forth. It was loose and about to come off, so he looked around for a place to land. He picked a big patch of tundra with a little frozen lake at the far end.

Smitty brought the plane down on the ice. It was equipped with skis, so it was an easy landing, coasting to a stop.

There was no radio on board, and in those days there wasn't too much concern if you didn't show up right on time. It would probably be about three days before search parties were sent to look for them.

Smitty and Clarence decided the best thing would be to walk out. Mudhole calculated they were about sixty miles from Chisana, where N.P. Nelson operated a little radio station.

Clarence was a natural outdoorsman and knew wilderness survival. There was plenty of survival equipment aboard the plane, including a five-gallon coffee can of emergency rations. When Kirk made up emergency rations, he filled them with cans of food, medical supplies and a pint of brandy or rum. He bought navy beans or rice in barrels and poured them in around the tin cans as packing. The five-gallon can was pretty heavy, but it was solid survival food.

They would wait till morning to start. In a matter of minutes, Clarence had a comfortable camp, and they gathered firewood from the dry timber in the area.

The two men were young and the whole thing had become an adventure with the roaring fire, and the dark night around them. They would keep the fire going all night.

They brought out the five-gallon can of emergency rations.

"Hey, here's some brandy!" Rhode exclaimed.

They uncorked the bottle and had a small snort. "Just hits the spot," they both agreed.

Smitty kept pulling cans out of the big container. When he was done, the beans and rice that had been used as packing remained. Peering into the big square can, he observed, "There must be five or six inches of this stuff in here." Smitty leaned against a deadfall, stretched his feet to the fire and took another sip of brandy.

"This is the life," said Clarence, putting another chunk of wood on the fire. The cheerful flames lit up the cold Alaskan night.

After a few moments Smitty said, "I've been thinking. That stuff is pretty bulky. I'll cook up the beans and rice right now. Then we can let it freeze, cut it into smaller pieces, and it'll be just right for carrying in our packs."

The two scooped up snow for water to put in the pot with the beans and rice. Every so often as the snow melted, they'd add more while watching the merry fire and sipping brandy.

Soon the rice and beans began to swell, rising high in the pot. Smitty stirred them with a stick and added more snow, but the soup continued to increase in volume. Smitty began to look around for something to take the overflow if it should run over. There wasn't much he could use.

The soup was done, but it had come within an inch of the top. Much relieved, Smitty set the can out on the snow and turned in.

Trouble during a flight often meant emergency repairs in the bush. This Stearman biplane carried the copper belt, symbol of the McCarthy extension of the Cordova Air Service.

The next morning dawned clear and cold.

"Must be forty or fifty below," said Mudhole, stamping his feet and waving his arms to get the circulation going. They huddled next to the fire and drank hot tea.

Clarence checked the can and came back carrying five gallons of hard-frozen bean and rice soup. With a little hot water over the outside and a few taps with a rock, the square block of frozen soup slid out onto the frosty tundra.

Smitty went to the plane and took out some tools. He set about cutting the bean and rice soup into smaller blocks that could be tucked alongside the canned goods in the packs. The two men started out for Chisana, their snowshoes leaving a trail across the tundra.

Mudhole was not used to walking on snowshoes, but he soon developed a good rhythm and they made fair time.

For five days they mushed cross-country before reaching Bonanza Creek and turning up to Bonanza. This spot was a deserted gold mining camp in winter and a sluice mining camp in the summer. They planned to spend the night in a cabin and go to Chisana the next day.

As they approached the cabin, they saw the door was off. It didn't look too inviting.

"What do you think, Smitty? Shall we stay here or try to go on to Chisana?"

"Well, Chisana is only about eleven miles farther. Kirk will be getting worried about us by now."

Rhode agreed. They set off again, on their snowshoes. As they approached Chisana they saw signs of people — trappers, mostly. To their relief the trapline trails were packed down.

At nine o'clock in the evening they finally saw the cabins at Chisana. It had been dark since two o'clock in the afternoon, but it was a bright night with the moon shining on the snow.

The cabin belonged to N.P. Nelson, who was asleep inside. Beating on the door, the two men roused N.P. awake. "Who's there?" demanded a sleepy voice.

"It's Smitty the pilot and Clarence Rhode. Let us in."

The door opened and N.P. peered at them in the light from a coal oil lamp. "Say, there was just a radio call about you this afternoon. Kirk called and wanted to know if I'd seen you anywhere around here."

The two weary hikers followed N.P. into the cabin, where the older man stirred up the fire in the drum stove. He turned on the radio and gave Cordova a call. To everyone's surprise, Kirk's voice came right back.

"You got anything?"

"They just walked in."

"No kidding? Let me talk to Smitty."

Smitty said, "We blew a cylinder. As near as I can tell, we're about ten, maybe fifteen miles from Horsefeld Lake. It's a good place to land, and the airplane's tied down. The wing covers and everything are on it, so I'm sure it's all right."

"Well, okay," said Kirk, "Bob and I will leave in the morning, and we'll go right on in there." Bob Clemence was a pilot and mechanic with Cordova Air Service.

The next day Kirk and Bob Clemence flew to where Smitty said the plane was and Clemence fixed the engine. Next morning they flew into Chisana, picked up the two men and flew them back to Cordova.

Smitty and Clarence Rhode went out again after the fur smugglers, and eventually arrested the trader at Tetlin. They flew him to Valdez where the only court in Alaska that could try him was. It was a round trip of thirteen hundred miles to capture one smuggler.

Early in 1938 Kirk secured a contract with Sears Roebuck to fly its packages and freight to Chitina and McCarthy in conjunction with the Post Office department. With Kirk's contract the company could ship one large package via the Alaska Steamship Company to Cordova. Cordova Air would open it and load the packages into the airplane for delivery. The packages were mostly shoe-box size, already addressed, and easy to handle. With six hundred people at the Kennecott mines and McCarthy, and probably another two hundred at Chitina, this was a very good account.

About the first of March, while the weather was still quite cold, Smitty loaded the Bellanca with packages from Sears, filling the back end and the aisle between the passengers.

There were three passengers for this trip: a sixteen-year-old boy headed for McCarthy, and a couple bound for a placer mine thirty miles out of McCarthy.

They boarded the plane. The man sat next to Smitty in the copilot's seat, and the woman and boy sat in seats behind them. The woman was quite heavy; the only way she could make the seat belt fasten was to take off the cushion and sit on the canvas underneath. When everyone was aboard, Smitty finished piling parcels in the aisle and around the folks' feet.

The plane was heated by exhaust. Connected to the exhaust system was a three-foot-long "blooey pipe" with a jacket welded tight around it. As air passed through this jacket, it was heated by the exhaust pipe. It then passed through a tube to the cabin outlets by ducts. One heat duct was under the lady's seat.

The heat control was a Bowden type, which consisted of a piece of steel piano wire through a thin flexible tube of tiny wire rings. It was unreliable, especially in cold weather when it would always stick. "They were a real headache," said Smitty.

He took off on his trip to McCarthy, a flight of an hour-and-a-half. In thirty minutes the woman began to complain that she was becoming too warm. The hot air from under her seat was trapped by the packages wedged around her. To top it off, there was no cushion under her, only the single piece of canvas.

Smitty reached down to turn off the Bowden control and spill the heat outdoors instead of inside. The control buckled in his hands, and he couldn't turn off the heat.

Another ten minutes went by, and she was complaining loudly again. Her husband tried to exchange seats with her, but with the packages jammed in the aisle and wedged among passengers, he had no room to move. The husband then tried to pull her out of her seat, so she could crawl over the back and into his, but she was too heavy. Smitty found himself fighting to control the airplane in a flurry of flying elbows and struggling bodies. After a few more minutes of wheezing, grunting and wrestling, they gave up.

Finally, she just had to make the best of it. They opened the side windows, which cooled everybody from the waist up, but from the waist down she was still roasting.

At last they arrived in McCarthy. When Mudhole landed she told him what she thought of the Cordova Air Service and of him personally as a pilot. She said she intended to examine herself and see how badly she was burned, and Cordova Air Service could rest assured they would be well sued for it.

She went to a friend's cafe-rooming house. It so happened that one of the boarders was not feeling well, and the proprietress was filling a hot water bottle when she heard the car drive up.

The proprietress laid the hot water bottle on one of the high stools at the counter and went out to meet the woman from the plane, who came in complaining loudly about the horrible trip she had had, and how she was burned. Could she use the bedroom to examine herself and see what damage had been done to her anatomy?

While she was talking she walked down the counter, put her feet up on the rungs of the stool and sat down on the bottle full of scalding water. It broke and she found herself sitting in a pool of boiling hot water.

Cordova Air Service was off the hook because there was no way to tell which burn was which. In time, she healed and the incident was forgotten.

Meanwhile, in January of 1938 Merle sent Bertha a ring.

"You know, it's really a small world," said Bertha, recalling it. "In our Ladies' Aid at church was a friend of mine, Ann Moore, who had a boyfriend in Sitka, teaching in the Sheldon Jackson School there. Ann got her engagement ring from Alaska on the same day I got mine." All mail was by ship in those days, so both rings came south from Alaska on the same boat.

It was planned that she should come north in the spring, and she and Smitty would be married.

Freight for the Mines

During the winter of 1937-38 a Mr. Zeltzer, former governor of New York, acquired mining property in the Horsefeld district, beyond the Chugach Mountains over in the White River country.

Mr. Zeltzer wanted to prospect a vein of ore and see if there was any chance of developing a productive gold mine. Kirk took the job of flying the necessary fifteen tons of equipment. It was shipped to McCarthy on the Copper River & Northwestern Railway. Smitty was to fly four to five hundred pounds at a time to Horsefeld during the month of May.

As May rolled around, Kirk arranged for Sam Gamblin to fly into the Horsefeld area and start cutting brush for at least a semblance of an airport.

Sam and Smitty flew there and Sam set up his camp. Smitty marked out an area seventy-five feet wide and some five hundred feet long for him to clear, a field that would handle a Bellanca.

Smitty returned to McCarthy. A few days later when he flew back to see the new Horsefeld airstrip, Smitty described it this way:

"Sam Gamblin, being more of a mining man than an airport builder, started out right, but when I flew down there a few days later, the airfield almost came to a point at the lower end. He got tired of cutting so much brush, I guess, and he kept narrowing it so the lower end was only wide enough to fit the wheels."

Flying fifteen tons of freight in a small open cockpit Stearman was an interesting experience. There was a lot of big mine equipment, often awkwardly loaded. It usually took some muscle to get it aboard, and Smitty found he had to impose on some miner friends around McCarthy and the Kennecott mine for help. Some of the husky Norwegians, like Ole Petersen and his brother Knute, could lift hundreds of pounds of mining equipment out of the plane all by themselves.

Long poles, tents and the like had to be strapped to the outside of the plane. One time Mudhole flew with a tent tied on the wing. About the middle of Skolai Pass he noticed that the tent was working loose from its wrappings and was gradually unfurling. Part of it had already come in under the leading edge of the wing.

"The tent was billowing out, and the airplane was flying sideways," recalled Smitty. "Just a little bit more of it out of the roll and I would have been floating on the end of a big long parachute, the tent. I sure wouldn't have been airborne any longer." He was a very relieved pilot when he landed that day at Horsefeld.

The seemingly fragile airplanes of that era were actually remarkably tough machines.

Up the rampaging Copper River, near the junction with the Chitina, is narrow, rock-sided Woods Canyon. Here and there a lone, tough tree grows, its roots burrowed into a crack in the rock face.

Smitty had noticed a large tree on the canyon wall; it grew out from the face at a forty-five degree angle. Its trunk bent at the base to send the tree upward. It was one of a thousand details of the river he had observed during his flights.

On this particular occasion, Smitty's assignment was to pick up some miners and their gear in McCarthy and fly them to Cordova.

When he arrived in McCarthy, ten inches of fresh heavy snow lay on the ground.

The Bellanca could carry six passengers and a big load of baggage. He put aboard four men, one woman, himself as pilot, and a lot of baggage.

When Smitty tried to take off in the wet heavy snow, he couldn't get up enough speed to be airborne. He had to turn around, stop, cool off the motor and get the sticky packed snow off the skis. While doing this, he received verbal abuse from the passengers, who had spent the summer isolated in the mine and were anxious to get to town. They made barbed remarks: "Why couldn't Cordova Air send us a *good* pilot?"

After a couple of tries to take off, Smitty was forced to lighten the load. He unloaded two of the men and their gear and tried again. Cordova Air Service was getting twenty-five dollars per passenger, so every person he pulled off cut the profit of the flight.

Still he couldn't get airborne. "I never did make it that day," he said, "and the owner blessed me up one side and down the other all evening in the hotel because of it.

"The next morning I got up before daylight, but it was about 10:30 A.M. when the weather seemed to break a little. I decided to get off, because I just couldn't stand much more of that chewing out. I took a lady and three men, and that time I was able to get off.

"As I got down the river it started to snow, so I slid over to the Chitina River and the next thing I knew I was flying down below the level of the river banks. The banks are high, forty to one hundred feet. As I got along toward Chitina I thought, well, I probably can get in there and land on the lake. It's right in town, and they had good places to stay in Chitina.

"So I went on. I came to the junction of the Chitina and Copper rivers, headed towards Cordova. I was sure that the farther I went toward Cordova, the better the weather would get.

"But as quick as you turn left from the Chitina toward the Copper River, you head into Woods Canyon, which is a ve-ery narrow canyon, not much wider than the wingspan of the Bellanca I was flying. Or so it seemed.

"In the canyon I was watching the left wall, keeping my wing out from there a little way, sure that I would then clear the right wall. Apparently I wasn't as close to the left wall as I thought. All at once the airplane almost stopped, and slewed around to the right. I thought I had hit the canyon wall, but the plane came loose after losing fifty feet and kept on flying.

"I came out of the canyon, and in a few miles the weather began to improve. I was able to lean over and look at the wing. The whole leading edge was collapsed.

"On landing in Cordova, I found the wing had hit something about four nose ribs back from the end. There was hardly a leading edge to the wing at all.

"The next day I took another airplane and went back to McCarthy. I flew low through the canyon to see what I hit. Sure enough it was that big old tree growing out from the canyon wall on the right side, and the whole top third of it was sheared off."

Mudhole figures that was about the closest call of his career.

"All in all, during that period of four or five years, I must have made a thousand trips up and down that Copper River," he said. "I got to know it real well. After that, I knew every bush and tree."

Flying freight to the mines was full of interesting little experiences. He took empty oil barrels back from the mines, and when the plane began its descent, the air pressure change would cause the drums to bang like a shotgun blast, making pilot and unwary passengers jump.

Smitty used the section houses to check on his weather ahead. Once a strange voice answered his call.

"Vot's dat you say," inquired a Scandinavian voice from a section house.

"What's your visiblity?" Smitty asked.

"Vot you mean?" came the slightly puzzled answer.

"The visibility. How far can you see?"

"I can't see notting."

"Well, how many telephone poles can you count?"

"Vell, I count von vonce in a vile."

"That's fine," said Smitty. "Now what's your ceiling?"

"Vot's dat?"

"What's your ceiling? What's above you?"

There was a moment of silence and then came the answer. "Ve-ell, I can't spell very goot, but I tink it says 'Celotex.' "

Weddings—Cordova Style

Smitty had never forgotten Bertha, the telephone operator in Nebraska who had put him in touch with Kirk in Alaska. They had kept in correspondence, and that led to romance. Bertha was to arrive on the *Yukon* in early April. Besides Smitty, only Kirk and his wife Dean knew she was coming.

About a week before Bertha was expected, Kirk had a call for a flight to Cape Yakataga. The beach at Cape Yakataga is a narrow strip of sand strung out between the ocean and the Bagley Icefield which feeds some of the continent's most magnificent glaciers for several hundred miles along the North Pacific coast. Between the glaciers and the beach the land is densely forested and enjoys a relatively mild climate. It is beautiful country, though it rains often.

Spring tends to be wet, chilly and miserable. Still, there have been a few people making their homes along this coast since time immemorial. Of attraction are the large runs of salmon, the gold-bearing sands of Cape Yakataga and the potentially fruitful oil fields. Gold comes and goes with the storms that pound the shoreline.

The beach is open to the full sweep of the stormy North Pacific Ocean. When the weather is fit for flying, the gulf surf is only a dull roar always in the ears of those who live there. The sand, pounded by the constant waves, is hard and good for landing a plane. But it is subject to freak waves, and here and there the runoff from the upland cuts sudden channels in the beach.

Among those living at Cape Yakataga were the two Dahlgren girls, Edna and Helen, married to Ben Watson and Mel Grindle, prospectors of the area.

The call for a flight to the cape came from Mrs. Dahlgren in Cordova, who said her husband was ill and not expected to live the night. She wanted her two daughters, Edna and Helen, brought to Cordova to see their father, probably for the last time.

Kirk dispatched Mudhole Smith in the Stearman, and called the cape by radio to let them know Smitty's expected time of arrival. He asked them to mark the beach where it was safe to land.

It was that raw, cold spring weather, and because the Stearman had an open cockpit, Smitty wore a huge, warm bearskin flying suit. In this protective outfit, with his beaver hat on his head, he took off for the cape at 4 P.M. It was April, and the sky would be light until eight o'clock.

As he came over the reef off Cape Yakataga, he saw the beach had been marked out for his landing by Ben Watson and Mel Grindle. He could be sure the sand was firm.

Edna and Helen, dressed in warm clothes, helmets, goggles and woolen neck scarves, waited nervously on the beach.

The one thing that Kirk had neglected to tell his pilot about was freak waves. Smitty had no experience in landing on ocean beaches.

His wheels touched the hard-packed sand, and he began coasting to a stop. Just then a big wave came crashing in, covering the wheels and flipping the plane over on its back.

Smitty hanged upside down by his safety belt as the water receded. He reached to release his belt and immediately tumbled out of the open cockpit onto his head. Then the second wave hit him. The bearskin flying suit was full of air, and as the second wave retreated, Smitty found himself floating helplessly out to sea.

Mel saw what was happening and ran into the water. He

grabbed Smitty by the collar and stopped his exodus till the wave was gone. Smitty flopped on the sand, soaked and shaken. The suit was now full of water and so heavy that he couldn't get up, even with Mel's help. And another wave was coming.

Smitty wriggled out of the suit, getting free just ahead of the wave. He and Mel ran for high ground while the last of the series of three waves buried Smitty's bearskin flying suit in sand. The plane was on its back, half covered with sand, with Smitty's treasured fur hat nearby.

The first job at hand was to get the plane to safe ground, above the high tide line. The next problem was to load the bearskin flying suit, sodden and full of sand, into the plane, a chore almost as bad as digging out the plane. After several hours of hard work, the plane was pulled to a safe spot. Helen and Edna, standing by, had cooked a good meal and placed a hot toddy in each man's hand. The beaver hat had been rescued and was hanged to dry.

That evening Smitty talked to Kirk on the radio, and the next morning Kirk flew to Cape Yakataga in the Bellanca and landed at low tide. He had brought with him a mechanic, John Foode, and a mechanic-pilot, Bob Clemence. The upper wings of the Stearman needed complete rebuilding, a job that would take several days.

Kirk knew Smitty was to be married in a few days, so he took the young pilot to Cordova with the Dahlgren girls. Unfortunately, their father had died during the night.

Bertha and Merle were married in April 1938. The wedding was one of the best-kept secrets in Cordova history. In a very small town everyone usually knows what's happening to everyone else.

Thinking back on it, Bertha feels the wedding was kept a secret because of the shivaree threat, a good old Cordova custom. In most places a shivaree is a mock serenade for newlyweds done with pots and pans. In Cordova, however, the groom might be kidnapped on his wedding night for a two-week fishing trip, or any number of such variations.

"Maybe Merle was instrumental in some of those past shivarees, and he knew what might happen," Bertha said. Dean had done a bang-up job of getting things ready. The ceremony was performed before an altar decked with burning tapers and festooned with hearts and bells. Decorations hung from various points to the center of the room. The Kirkpatricks were best man and matron of honor, and the only ones present beside the bride, groom and minister.

A modest reception followed at 8 P.M., with a small coterie of friends, none of whom knew beforehand who the bride and groom were to be.

Someone from the reception went downstairs to the Lathrop Theatre and placed an announcement on the screen. That was how Cordova got the news. As a result, the newlyweds had their shivaree after all, with everyone appearing outside the Smith's apartment door beating on pans, pounding on the door and making the appropriate racket in honor of the new couple.

All in all, it was an exciting first day in Alaska for Bertha, the newly arrived bride.

ALASKA FLIER

Kirkpatrick's Repair Shop

In many ways, Cordova Air Service was Kirkpatrick. Harold Gillam began flying more or less regularly out of Cordova before Kirk came, but as he moved into the Interior of Alaska, most of his coastal flying around Cordova was subcontracted to Kirkpatrick.

Kirk had already been associated with Gillam's flying service when he, along with a number of local businessmen, formed Cordova Air Service in 1934. Many of the businessmen had associations with the Copper River & Northwest Railway, which ran from Cordova to the rich Kennecott copper mines. Most of the stockholders of Cordova Air Service were also stockholders in independent mining ventures in the Copper River valley and the Kennicott-McCarthy area. It was a rich gold and copper area, and their main concern when forming Cordova Air Service was to keep mine employees happy with regular mail and fresh groceries.

Kirk was a good pilot, but he was an even better mechanic. Under his management, Cordova was probably the finest aircraft repair shop in Alaska. It was built originally by Cap Lathrop in 1934, and was one of only two or three in the territory that was government accredited. The tiny Eyak Lake airstrip was a mecca for Alaska bush fliers when they had ailing aircraft.

The field was in a bowl surrounded by mountains. The little strip was built along the edge of the lake and was only a few feet higher than the water. Landings were made in summer either on pontoons on the lake or with wheels on the gravel strip, and in winter with skis on the ice or on the snow-covered strip. It had floatplane facilities for docking and for hoisting off the water, as well as hangars and the repair shop.

Because of its precarious location, landings could be hairy at that field. John Cross was an early flier in Alaska who brought Kirk's first Bellanca to Alaska. He didn't fly it north, but put it on an Alaska steamship and came along "just to take a look around Alaska."

Cross said, "I saw what was going on and it was seven years before I got back to the States. Things were really popping in the aircraft industry. There wasn't much industry, but there was a world of chance for it. Kirkpatrick had set up a shop in Cordova and that was really necessary because everybody was wrecking airplanes as fast as they were flying them. There were no fields worthy of the name."

Eyak Field was a favorite spot of the bush pilots, although its location among mountains and along a lake made landings there somewhat adventurous. Pictured is the Cordova Air Service shop at Eyak Field at high water.

Cross told of a landing on Eyak Lake at night, and of course, there were no lights. He could see where he was by the dark shadow of the surrounding mountains, but little else. As he approached, he switched on the landing lights. There, right in front of him, was a rowboat.

He managed to miss the boat, but it was a hair-raising experience. That one of the kids in the rowboat was his own didn't help matters a bit.

Ray Petersen recounts another of the hazards. He landed a Travel Air, which was on wheels, on the ice. He intended to land on the gravel strip, but his arrival timing was a bit off, and as he got over Hinchinbrook Island, it was getting dark.

He had never landed on the Eyak Field before, but on a boat trip he had taken time to walk over and look at it, so he had the general idea of the layout — the way the railroad tracks ran along one side of the lake, and how the airport was chiseled out of the mountainside. "For a guy used to flying in the Midwest, it was a bit hair-raising," he said, "but at least I knew what the general layout was.

"So I came in over town, and by this time it was very dark. Except for the lights of the hangar — they had the doors open — the lake was like an inkwell. I didn't give it too much thought because I didn't think it was too bad a deal. I flew up the lake, made a 180, and I could see the lights of the railroad roundhouse. I knew that was close to the end of the lake. I made the landing all right — went bouncing along on the lake and taxied up to the ramp.

"Our old friend Kirk came out and said: 'How in the devil did you do that? Even Harold Gillam don't fly in conditions this bad.'

"I said, 'Well, I didn't see much wrong with it.'

"And Kirk replied, 'Yeah? What I mean is, how'd you keep from falling into the lake? The ice is melting and it's full of holes.' "

Bill Egan, later to become first governor of Alaska after statehood, was a Valdez lad who flew an Aeronca. On a number of occasions, Egan would fly to Cordova for dinner and a show.

He recounts that after one such trip, "I went out and headed for Valdez. It was foggy out over town, but I thought after I got past Hawkins Island it would open up. Just about the time I thought the fog would lift, the engine quit on one cylinder. The real significance of that was the plane had only three cylinders.

"I whirled it around in the fog, went back into the field and landed the quickest way I could — downwind. It was vibrating something awful, so I cut the switch.

"It was early in the morning and no one was around. I taxied off the field to the hangar, and sat there revving it up. Not a spit or sputter, but I knew something was wrong.

"When Kirk, Smitty and a fellow named Souca — that was in 1939 — came in, I told them what had happened.

"We wheeled the airplane into the hangar. They took the carburetor off, but I kept telling them that I didn't think it was the carburetor. So they worked on the ignition, and after that on whatever else they thought it could be. They worked all day, and when they put it back together, it ran great.

"The next morning I took off. It was running good until I got out of sight of town. Suddenly, one cylinder quit again.

"I wheeled it around and headed back. I wanted to land as quick as I could, so I did it downwind again.

"I taxied off the field, and just as I was opening the hangar door, I heard Smitty say, 'You know, that kid better learn to quit that downwind landing or he's going to kill himself.'

"Well, I had them work on it again. No one heard it when it was acting up, and they looked at me like I had rocks in my head because it ran so well on the ground.

"Next morning I took off and got out past town. Sure enough, it quit as soon as I was out of sight. It was vibrating something awful, so I came back and landed downwind again.

"Smitty came up to me and said, 'Let me try that.' He took the airplane up, and I thought, 'Sure as the devil the engine will work now.' We watched till he was just a speck in the distance. I was thinking, 'Now, he'll come back and say there's nothing wrong.'

"All of a sudden we saw a violent maneuver — the airplane went sideways, and I think he did a roll. He came back and landed — downwind!"

The trouble was diagnosed as a sticky valve, and Egan was off the hook for his downwind landings. They might have been stumped for a while that time, but Egan says Kirk's shop was the best, always going a little bit farther than necessary to be helpful.

Last Train from McCarthy

About a month after his marriage Smitty was transferred to McCarthy to form a subsidiary of Cordova Air Service called Airways, Inc., the "Copper Belt Line." Planes for this branch of the business had a large copper colored belt painted around the fuselage.

He and Bertha rented a small furnished house from Kate Kennedy for ten dollars a month. Kate was originally from Dawson City. She had moved to McCarthy in 1914 and opened a hotel. She had been there since, and had acquired a one-bedroom house which the young couple moved into.

The little house had a wood stove and Bertha learned to cook on it. Her first loaf of homemade bread came out so well she took a picture of it.

That fall she went on berry-picking expeditions with the local women. These trips took place by train — they rode to a good spot near the Iversons' farm and picked all day. There were blueberries and low-bush cranberries, which made wonderful pies, jams and other goodies. Bertha had plenty to cook on her wood stove.

Smitty continued to wear his warm beaver hat on his flights. Bertha was aware of the hat's origin, but was a happy new bride and an intelligent woman. She said nothing about it.

One time, flying down the Copper River in the Bellanca, Smitty ran into snow and ice. The plane had a big sliding window on the side, which allowed the pilot to lean over and peer out when the front window was covered with snow and ice. Smitty leaned out, and his hat flew off. He felt pretty sad about it because he knew he'd never see it again.

When he landed in Cordova, he picked up the tail to pull the plane into the hangar. There was the hat, hanging on a strut. The only damage was a torn earflap.

Bertha was prepared to accept the hat, but she wasn't prepared to go so far as to repair it. Smitty couldn't get the earflap sewn back on, and it looked rather shabby after that, so he didn't wear it quite so often.

Eventually the hat disappeared. Being a happy husband and a prudent man, Smitty asked no questions.

Years later, when bush pilot portraits were commissioned by Bob Reeve and painted by Harvey Goodale, Mudhole Smith was painted wearing his treasured beaver hat.

McCarthy, Chitina, Kennicott and Cordova were railroad towns, all concurrent with the building of the Copper River & Northwestern Railway. Copper had been pouring out of the mines near Kennicott in fantastic amounts during the 1910s and 1920s. The general depression of the early thirties hit the copper industry as well as every other business, and new copper discoveries in Chile offered less expense and more profit to companies. The Kennicott mines and mills were in a state of decline. The railroad, owned by the people of Kennecott Copper Company, was now operated only in the summers. This was good for flying during the winter months, but in summer when flying was easy, business was off because of the availability of ground transportation.

The last train left Kennicott in the late fall of 1938 and came through McCarthy on its trip south. The townspeople hoped that perhaps it was quitting just for the winter, as it had for the past five years. They felt it might start running again in the spring of 1939, even though the company had applied for a Certificate of

Convenience and Necessity to terminate the service, the formal step necessary to close the line.

It was a snowy day in November as that train pulled into McCarthy. Some women were crying. It was a sad occasion, except for Smitty. He figured that those people had only two ways in or out: walk or fly. In his naivete, he thought he had it made.

"I began to find out right away that when the economy folds, you go right with it," he explained ruefully. Other business had to be found to replace it.

Earlier that summer he had gone to Chisana, a thriving community, and stayed overnight. Karl Killian, a miner and trapper from the area, walked up to the Bonanza Mine with him to keep the bears away. Smitty talked to the miners and made a deal to fly all the freight in the winter of 1938 and spring of 1939, which was the first business Cordova Air Service had with Chisana. Apparently the miners were satisfied with the service, because it became one of the mainstays of Cordova Air Service in the next few years.

For Bertha it was a happy winter, although McCarthy was very small after the closing of the railroad. Only four of the resident women stayed. There was Mary Pytel, Ilou O'Neill, Mrs. Jack Shultz and Marian Fitzgerald. Anna Iverson, who lived on a farm, was there, but she came in only once in a while. The women got together often, and made a pleasant time of the winter.

The incredible scenic grandeur of the Wrangell Mountains and the spectacular setting of the Kennecott mines were already attracting the attention of the Interior Department and others. The closing of the Kennecott mines was causing great concern in Chitina, McCarthy and Cordova, all heavily dependent on mining. Especially devastating was the closure of the Copper River & Northwestern Railway.

Ernest Gruening was associated with the Interior Department, and he made several trips to Alaska to learn firsthand the problems of the northern territory. Having seen the Wrangell Range, he decided it was National Park caliber.

The dramatic setting of the Kennecott mines and mill, rising up the steep side of the mountain high above the glacier and river valley, would make it a natural for conversion into a hotel. It would attract people from all over the world, he was sure. It also would make it feasible to keep the Copper River & Northwestern Railway running.

The problem, of course, was that no one knew whether the Kennecott people would release or sell the property.

One day Mudhole got a telephone call telling him that Gruening and his party would be arriving in McCarthy and wanted to do some flying. Smitty was to give them the best service he could.

On the day of the flight, Gruening showed up with one of his sons, two men from the Interior Department, and the head of the Alaska Road Commission. The party filled the seats in the Bellanca.

The first day they flew up the Chitina River and over Chitina Glacier, then on to Canada and the Donjek area. They came back up the White River and down through Chitistone Pass, returning to McCarthy for the night.

About seven o'clock the next morning the Bellanca took off for a day of spectacular sightseeing from the air. Mudhole figured if he had to gas, he could do it at Copper Center.

First they flew through the Skolai Pass, over the bustling little mining community of Chisana, on to the Tanana Flats near Northway and then back over Chisana River. From the vicinity of Chisana they climbed to twelve thousand feet, over the tops of most of the peaks. Even at that altitude, though, there were a number of mountains higher than the plane. It was an incredible panorama of high peaks and valleys filled with snow and blue-white glaciers.

One of the passengers was so delighted, he was taking pictures through an open window of the plane. The windows in the rear did not slide, but the photographer found that they would open slightly when pushed. So one of the passengers sat down and pressed his feet on the plexiglas window, pushing it out against the slipstream while the other took pictures. It made the plane harder to fly, but Smitty was giving the VIPs the red carpet treatment, so he didn't object.

About halfway across the tall mountains, Mudhole looked out his window to see black smoke pouring from an exhaust pipe.

His blood ran cold for a moment. Something was wrong with the engine. All around him was the roughest kind of country, and jagged peaks as far as he could see. Just the thought of a forced landing with all these "wheels" aboard made him shudder.

The oil pressure light began to flicker.

Smitty told the passengers not to push the window out, that it made the airplane hard to handle. None of the passengers saw the smoke, but they accepted his order.

The engine wasn't missing or acting up in any way, so he decided not to worry his passengers by telling them the problem.

Instead, he headed straight for Copper Center, saying it was lunch time.

They were still at a high altitude as they approached Copper Center, some forty minutes later. The temperature gauge was climbing, showing that the engine was running too hot because of an oil shortage. The oil pressure light glowed red.

He made a slow letdown to the Copper Center field, a field fifteen hundred feet long. The strip was across from Grandpa McCrary's small farm, and as the Bellanca rolled to a stop, the old man drove over in his Model A truck to meet It. McCrary met every plane.

Mudhole and the passengers piled into the truck, most of them in the back. Smitty didn't say anything about the engine trouble to his passengers, but he did ask McCrary if he had any airplane oil.

"Don't have a bit," he said cheerfully. "But I'll tell you what I do have. I've got a whole fifty-gallon barrel that the boys put their oil in when they drain their engines in the wintertime." Gillam and other pilots dumped their oil into a barrel instead of onto the snow.

The Model A bumped down the dusty road to the old Copper Center Roadhouse. Mrs. Lawrence, the proprietress, fixed lunch for the guests.

Mudhole went into the kitchen and told her that he had a little engine trouble. "Nothing serious, but I don't want to worry the others. Will you make me a quick sandwich so I can sneak on out and fix it while the rest are eating?"

She obliged, and when Smitty took his sandwich, he cautioned her not to mention where he was going. McCrary drove him back to the airstrip to get the oil barrel. Mudhole measured the airplane's oil reserve and found the tank almost empty, hardly more than a gallon left.

Mudhole calculated his distance to McCarthy. He knew how long he'd been in the air when he first discovered the smoke, but he didn't know how long it had been smoking before he noticed. Not too long, he guessed. His figures indicated he could make it back to McCarthy with no real trouble. He hoped he was right.

The two men rolled the barrel over onto a box and poured oil into a gallon bucket for draining into the airplane. Mudhole filled the engine with the old, black used engine oil.

Meanwhile, his passengers came walking to the airfield, enjoying the fine weather, fresh air and the chance to stretch their legs. When they got into the plane, Gruening asked, "Where are we going now, pilot?"

Smitty hedged the question a bit. "Well, I think we'd better go to McCarthy. I'm not sure my engine is running as good as I want it to."

"O.K. Are you sure we're not in any serious trouble?"

"No, no. Some little thing. I'll have to get my wrenches and stuff and then I can fix it." They accepted this story.

Fifteen minutes out of Copper Center the engine began heating again, and Mudhole could see the smoke once more. But, as he had figured, they made it into McCarthy with no real trouble. There was still half a tank of oil left.

He had a good idea of what was wrong. The supercharger had gone out. The load in the plane, combined with the altitude, and maybe a little extra strain on the engine with the window being pushed out for photographs, combined to make the engine pull pretty hard. The bearings were out on the supercharger, he was sure. That's where the oil was coming from, entering the induction system and out the exhaust.

Smitty and Kirk had a radio code for talking to Cordova when they didn't want anyone to overhear what they were saying. Smitty called Cordova, using the code to tell what had happened and asking for advice.

Kirk didn't bother to code the answer. He said, "Keep the plane there on the ground. I'll bring Carl [the mechanic] up in the morning."

Early the next morning the two men appeared. Carl Baehr tore the engine down at McCarthy field and put in new superchargers. Smitty was impressed because a year later the engine was still running well.

Meanwhile the Gruening entourage moved on to new sights in its tour of Alaska. Smitty still gets goose flesh when he thinks of trying for a forced landing with that important party from Washington, D.C.

He had better luck flirting with the high mountains when he flew Bradford Washburn, the famous mountaineer-photographer-scientist, on an aerial expedition to the flanks of Mounts Logan, Walsh and Lucania.

It was October and the flight lasted three hours and twenty minutes. The weather and light for photography were perfect, and Washburn was ecstatic over the quality of the pictures he was able to obtain. Washburn said the flights along the south and east sides of Mt. Lucania were the most difficult because of the incredibly wild nature of the country, with no place to land in case of trouble.

Smitty had to call on all his skills to put Washburn in just the right place to get the right ingredients in his pictures — close enough to the mountains for the detail to show, yet far enough for proper perspective. Washburn was highly complimentary of Mudhole's flying.

With the mines closed since the fall before, about the first of March only a few persons were left in McCarthy. Kirk and Smitty discussed the situation and decided Smitty should transfer to Copper Center and use it as the base of operations. There was a lot of business there, mostly taking freight to the mines. The freight came as far as Copper Center on trucks and had to be flown from the highway to the mines.

Smitty went to Copper Center, found a house and paid the first month's rent. Then he got a job offer from his friend Noel Wien.

Wien Air Service was operating out of Nome, where a small boom was in progress. There was a lot of mining equipment on the beach at Teller to be taken into the Interior in Wien's Ford Trimotor. It paid on a percentage basis, and Smitty's calculations told him that he could be making as much as a thousand dollars a month.

He almost promised Noel that he would take the job, but he still had to talk to Kirk, who had raised his wages during the winter to $250 a month.

On the morning of April 10, 1939, Kirk flew up to McCarthy with a load of miners for Dan Creek. While he was there, he and Mudhole discussed the future. Smitty, of course, had told him of the job offer at Nome. Kirk offered him another fifty dollars a month to stay on with Cordova Air. Smitty promised to think it over.

Kirk took off in the Bellanca with a passenger, Con Miller of McCarthy, with uncertain weather down the Copper River. The McCarthy airport was half a mile from the old strip, and Smitty walked home deep in thought. He hated to leave Kirk, but the offer from Wien was a very good one, and he felt he probably would accept it.

When he got home, Bertha was visiting with friends. The weather had closed in, and it was beginning to snow rather heavily. Smitty turned on the two-way radio and talked once more to Kirk. Kirk reported that he was someplace down around Allen Glacier near Mile 63.

That was near the limit of radio range to talk to Smitty, and from Allen Glacier he usually began to contact Cordova instead.

The signals were getting bad as Smitty listened, static crackled over the set, and the reception was very poor. He did manage to hear Cordova give the weather report to Kirk — zero-zero and blowing, heavy snow. After that he lost contact with Kirk.

Smitty poured a cup of coffee and sat back to wait. With the weather report in mind, Smitty halfway expected Kirk to be back to McCarthy. Flying down the Copper River would be impossible.

For half an hour or better, poor reception and static kept Smitty from hearing anything. It was getting close to noon, and Smitty was becoming uneasy. He stayed by the radio trying to call Cordova.

Finally the signals cleared for five minutes and Smitty was able to contact Lawrence Barr at Cordova.

Smitty asked, "Where's Kirk now? Did he get into Cordova, or is he on his way back here?"

Barr answered, "We don't know. We haven't heard from him."

"Well, what did he do after Mile 63?"

"He went back up the Copper River and said he was coming down Nelson River."

If he was flying down Nelson River, that meant he was coming into Cordova over Orca Inlet and would be flying over water the last fifteen or twenty miles of the trip.

Smitty said, "Maybe he's gone into Valdez." Valdez had no radio, so he suggested to Barr that he send a wire to Owen Meals in Valdez and find out if Kirk was there.

But in his mind, Smitty already knew that if Kirk had landed at Valdez he would immediately have sent a wire. The Alaska Communications System was good and sent messages promptly. Cordova would surely have received the word within fifteen minutes.

It had been nearly two hours since Smitty had talked to Kirk at Mile 63. He knew with a sick feeling what the answer from Valdez would be.

The Search

Smitty was still by the radio an hour or so later when the signals cleared again, and he was able to talk to Cordova.

"We heard from Valdez, and they say he isn't there."

While the signals were in, Smitty called Chitina and talked to Harry Moore. Kirk wasn't there, either.

By now, Smitty was sure there was a search to be made. He went out and looked up an old-timer, Harry Boyden, a guide. Boyden, who lived about four blocks away, knew everything necessary about wilderness survival.

Smitty told Boyden of Kirk's trouble and that he planned to take off as soon as possible to search for him.

"Can I get you to go with me?" he asked Boyden.

Boyden was anxious to go along, and immediately put together a pack of emergency gear. It was a large pack, because Smitty told Boyden they would probably stay in some house or cabin, or camp out, and they weren't coming back until they found Kirk.

It was nearly 3 P.M. when Mudhole Smith and Harry Boyden took off. Smitty had talked to Cordova, and Lawrence Barr suggested he look on Swan Glacier, and that he, Lawrence, would search the Nelson River.

Swan Glacier was a pass the pilots flew to drop from the Copper River valley into the Nelson River valley. As soon as Smitty was airborne, communications with Cordova improved. Lawrence and Smitty could then map out their search strategy.

As Smitty's Stearman headed up Swan Glacier, the snow squalls moved in thick and heavy. In moments, the pilot ran into a whiteout, that loss of horizon that occurs when earth and sky are white and give no point of reference. There seemed no way through, so Smitty turned back. Visibility was near zero till he came down off the glacier. The trees and brush along the river showed up black in the thick blowing snow.

He flew low, following the brush down the Tasnuna River toward the Copper River. When he crossed the railroad track he knew he was on the Copper River at Mile 83, and that directly ahead was a big lake near a trackwalker's shack. He continued through the swirling snow till he passed the shack, and then, drawing from experience, chopped the power and dropped onto the lake, which he couldn't see till he was right on it.

The plane was on skis, but the fresh powdered snow was piled deep, and rose to the Stearman's wings. For the last fifty feet it was pushing snow as it came to a halt.

Because of Harry Boyden's care, they had snowshoes and all the other equipment they might need. The men climbed out and put on the snowshoes. The plane was almost buried in the powdered snow, but there was no better position for it. It was protected from the high winds of the area and didn't even have to be tied down. Smitty told Boyden to pull the antenna out of the tail and hold it as far back behind the plane as he could. Then he called Cordova to say he was all right and tell where he was. The signals were bad, and he couldn't hear an answer if there was one. Later he found out that they had picked up the message.

Smitty and Boyden went into the trackwalker's shack, and while Harry was stoking up the fire, Smitty cranked the telephone on the wall furiously, hoping the line would work. The entire Copper River Railroad, 196 miles of it, was on a single telephone line of doubtful integrity, and the railroad had not run all winter. The railroad company, when it closed, left stoves, cooking utensils and other survival gear at all the trackwalker's shacks and section houses for the benefit of trappers and others who might need them, so the shack was well suited for spending the night. But the telephone did not raise any response.

The two of them ate, talked a little, and then went to bed. Early in the morning the telephone rang, much to the surprise of the two snowbound fliers.

Smitty got up and answered it.

"Hello. Who's this?" asked a voice.

"It's Smitty, the pilot. Who are you?"

"This is Earl Means, in Cordova. I was just trying to ring the hangar, down on Eyak Lake. Where are you?"

"I'm at the trackwalker's cabin at Mile 83. Harry Boyden is here with me."

Earl Means was one of the stockholders in Cordova Air Service, so Smitty and Earl carried on a long conversation, with both of them bringing the other up to date on the progress of the search, which was for the most part stalled because of the heavy snow and drifting squalls.

"Well, now, Smitty, you stay there until the weather clears. Don't do anything foolish. Don't *you* get in trouble, too."

"No, I won't," Smitty assured him. "I'll start out when the weather lets up, and if I don't contact anyone to let them know, I plan to fly straight down the Copper River and into Cordova that way."

"That's fine," Earl said. "You can gas up here and we'll do the searching from Cordova. Take care."

The two hung up, and Smitty went back to bed.

It was about 1 P.M. the next afternoon before the snow let up enough for Smitty and Boyden to take off. Once in the air, radio contact with Cordova was established, and the Cordova station told Smitty there had been a report of a plane heard flying low near Twin Lakes. Three persons living there had heard it fly over, and when they came to town, reported the fact. Smitty was asked to check it out.

Twin Lakes was near the head of Simpson Bay, and therefore, not too far distant from the Nelson River area where Kirk was last thought to have been. Lawrence Barr turned over the radio to someone else and joined Smitty and Boyden in the search. They spent the rest of the day looking in all the likely places where Kirk could have made a forced landing, but they found nothing.

"When I came back in," Smitty said, "I was sure he wasn't going to be found alive. Every place that he could have made a landing, he just wasn't there, and he knew this country real well." It was a heartsick crew that gave up the search when darkness came on.

By this time, dozens of fishing boats had joined the effort, searching both banks of Orca Inlet just below where Nelson River emptied into it.

On Sunday morning, as the searchers ate breakfast and awaited a break in the weather to get into the air, a fisherman named Joe Olson brought in a fragment of a plane. Smitty looked it over and identified it as the right aileron of the Bellanca which Kirk had been flying.

The fragment told a tragic story: The fabric was torn in several places and there were evergreen needles inside. The plane must have crashed through trees and fallen into the water.

The searchers were soon in the air again, combing Orca Inlet. The weather was greatly improved by now, and they began to fly low over the water, looking into the depths to try to spot the orange plane.

Meanwhile, the fishing boats taking part in the search were trying some new techniques. Otto Tiedeman, in his boat *Debs,* had spent the night rigging it with a new design of grappling and dragging gear made from a piece of three-inch galvanized pipe eighteen feet in length. Specially designed grapplers were attached.

Wednesday morning, Tiedeman and his crew set out again on the search. Early in the day, they spotted oil bubbles on the water. Tiedeman saw they were floating on a fast tide and estimated where they came from. He planted a buoy. He was within two hundred feet of the plane's location. The grapplers hooked the plane on the third try, in about ten fathoms. The *Debs* towed the wreckage to a shallow bay nearby, where divers from another boat went down to look it over. The two men were found inside.

The Bellanca was intact except for the right wing, which had been torn off. The plane evidently struck trees with the right wing, slewed around and crashed into the water.

The grim five-day search was over.

L.D. LaGassa, a deep-sea diver, secured lines around the wreckage and it was raised by a pile-driver tied up alongside LaGassa's boat *Polar Bear*.

The bodies of M.D. Kirkpatrick and his passenger, Con Miller, were brought to Cordova for funeral services.

Ila Dean Kirkpatrick returned to Wichita with the body of her husband. It was with great sadness that Cordova said goodbye.

Cordova Air Service's Mudhole Smith

Merle wired Noel Wien immediately after Kirk's plane was found, saying that in view of the tragedy he felt he could not now take the job he had been offered. The board of directors of Cordova Air Service had asked Smitty to stay on until they figured out what to do.

The year after Kirk's death the board elected Mudhole Smith president and general manager of the company, and he accepted.

Mudhole took stock of the situation, and it could hardly have been more bleak. He was now the only pilot on the job. Cordova Air Service had lost their best plane when Kirk went down, and the one Smitty had been flying was ready to go to California for a recovering job and an overhaul that couldn't be put off any longer.

Tom Donohue, the company attorney, had used the open cockpit Stearman during the search for Kirk, and since it was an unfamiliar plane to him, he ground-looped it on landing. The Stearman also was temporarily out of commission. The Pacemaker Bellanca was all that was left to fly.

At the same time, the demise of the Copper River & Northwestern Railway was beginning to show its effect in a depressed economy.

His great task, beyond the overhaul and recommissioning of planes, was to hire other pilots. The first one put on the payroll was a former World War I pilot named Jack Hewson, who had been flying out of Fairbanks on a hit or miss basis. He was a good pilot who was happy to get regular work.

Smitty implemented the plan he and Kirk had made to open the Copper Center base. He sent Hewson there while Smitty handled the Cordova end of it. He admits to being more of a pilot at heart than a businessman. As half of the flight team, he was frequently logging three trips to McCarthy and back in a day's time.

Within a few months Smitty managed to get his planes back in service, and even to expand a little by the purchase of a new Travel Air 6000.

Soon after buying the Travel Air, Smitty had occasion to remember his days of listening to tailspin stories, particularly the one told by Clarence Norton, the pilot who sprained his ankle reversing the controls on a low-level spin.

Mudhole was taking off from Eyak Field one morning in the Travel Air with four passengers and baggage bound for Katalla and Capl Yakataga. He had climbed to two hundred feet when one of the passengers yelled, "Smoke!"

Smitty looked around and smoke was pouring out from under the baggage.

The old Travel Airs had a rudimentary heater, a jacket around the exhaust stack which heated the air passing over the hot exhaust. The warm air ran into the cabin through a flexible tube.

A young mechanic's helper, in washing the grease off the airplane and giving it its check, had used a non-flammable solvent and spilled some into the heater pipe. When Smitty took off, it sent up a cloud of smoke that poured into the cabin.

Unaware of the real cause of the smoke, Smitty had not the slightest doubt that the plane was on fire. He wheeled the Travel Air around laying in on its side for a hard right turn back to the field.

Under the circumstances he gave no thought to the wind, and came in downwind. He was also too high. It hadn't been too long since he was doing aerobatic flying in the states, and he automatically pulled the Travel Air's nose up and then put her into a tight left slip to kill his speed. That did it.

The plane started to roll over on its right wing, and fell off into a sloppy spin. The plane began a corkscrew descent.

The story of Clarence Norton's plane flashed into his head and he found his reactions made to order. He jammed the controls forward, and opened the throttle wide at the same time, tightening the spin and gaining the speed necessary to recover. Then he quickly hit the left rudder and rolled the wheel hard left to give opposite aileron.

The spin stopped and the plane, now in a dive, was picking up speed.

"All at once I could feel I had flying speed and I pulled it up. The field at Eyak Lake was about two feet above the lake level and there were six guys watching me. There was Long Shorty, and Lawrence Barr and some of the mechanics, and they swore to a man that my wheels were below the level of the field, so I figure I missed the water by a foot.

"If I hadn't sat there that Sunday afternoon and listened to Raymond Hedrick tell about Clarence Norton, I certainly doubt if I would have done what I did then."

Bush service included all sorts of shipments. One day the boat arrived in Cordova with some freight consigned via Cordova Air Service to J.A. Fageberg at Long Lake, about 18 miles from McCarthy. The bill of lading read: "One live goat; one sack feed; feed three times daily."

Lawrence Barr, whom everybody called "The General," confined the goat in the hangar to await shipment.

Cordova Times, editorializing on the event, published a little ditty: "Smitty had a little goat, a little goat had he; and everywhere that Smitty and the General went, that goat they were sure to scent."

"The goat, a comely-looking, cream-colored creature and potential father of future Fageberg goats, is quartered in the dope room at the hangar, where his odors mingle with those of pigments and banana oil and thus aren't so offensive to his temporary caretakers, chief of whom is 'General' Lawrence Barr."

Smitty's new Travel Air was available, but no doubt remembering the incident of the cows in the back pastures of Kansas and their predilection for fabric, Smitty ferried the goat to Fageberg in his older Bellanca aircraft.

The bush pilots were great for figuring simple but ingenious ways of doing things. They devised a novel method of delivering mail to isolated cabins where there was no need to land except to deliver a single letter or message.

The message was simply tucked into the cardboard tube center of a roll of "bathroom stationery," a long streamer of the tissue pulled up through the center, and the message tossed from the window of the plane.

The trapper turned his eyes skyward to see the missive plummeting earthward, with a long white streamer to mark its fall. Easy to find, nicely weighted for its fall, and the message protected

Instead of landing to deliver an occasional letter to a camp, pilots offered a true "air" mail service, dropping letters inside rolls of toilet tissue. The tissue provided a streamer to break its own fall.

by the soft layers of tissue and the cardboard tube — who could ask for better service? Even the roll of tissue could be salvaged for use by the isolated trapper.

Although the closing of the railroad had depressed the economy, Cordova Air Service began to find new business to replace it. The trip to Chisana soon was as lucrative as the old Cordova-Chitina-McCarthy run had been.

"The closing of the railroad didn't hurt us as much as we thought it would," Smitty said. "We changed our tactic, our whole method of doing business. We did more flying from Cordova to Bristol Bay in the summer with the commercial fishermen, and we just tried a little harder."

By July of 1939 Cordova Air Service had inaugurated a new

weekly service to Chitina and McCarthy, flying that route on Fridays. To promote business in the area, flying trips to Tebay Lakes were offered. Rainbow trout could be caught there by the basketful, and soon many people were flying to Tebay Lakes for the fishing.

Cordova Air Service began flying more often to Anchorage, and they developed a semi-scheduled service to points on Prince William Sound, which had to be flown on floats.

In August of 1939, Mudhole Smith, V.G. Vance and Carl Baehr, mechanic at the Eyak Lake shop, bought the stock belonging to Ila Dean Kirkpatrick, Kirk's widow. With Baehr as chief mechanic, the excellence of the repair shop was maintained.

Although most pilots didn't know it, there were great changes ahead, that summer of 1939. Little noticed and not understood at all for its ramifications was a bill that the Congress of the United States had passed the year before — the Civil Aeronautics Act of 1938. In 1939 the newly appointed Civil Aeronautics Board (CAB) came to Alaska to hold hearings and make recommendations that would change flying in Alaska, as well as in the rest of the United States.

The Civil Aeronautics Board

In August of 1939 Smitty received a notice from Tom Donohue about impending Civil Aeronautics Board hearings in Alaska. The CAB examiner, Ray Stowe, was to explain the new law to all the Alaska operators. Scheduled flights were to be established, routes designated and assigned, and subsidies paid to airlines to assure that schedules were kept and strict safety standards were maintained. Mail contracts were to be a part of the total package.

For years, Alaska flight operators had been bidding on annual mail contracts and losing money on them. By 1939, about the only ones to bid on the mail contracts were those who were far-sighted enough — like Harold Gillam — to see what the Civil Aeronautics Act of 1938 might actually bring about.

The CAB team arrived in Seward by ship and boarded the train to Anchorage for the first of a series of hearings. Tony Dimond notified aviators all over Alaska, and a large group converged on Anchorage in late August.

The fliers, although they were all friends and shared much in common, were really isolated from one another most of the time. Fliers from Nome, for example, seldom saw fliers from Cordova. When the whole group got together in Anchorage for the hearings, it was like Old Home Week.

Smitty described what happened: "Here we all were in Anchorage, and we were all friendly and we had a lot to talk about. The manager of Star Airlines, Don Goodman, had a large apartment in the Anchorage Hotel, so he invited us all up there that night at eight o'clock to talk this thing over and see what kind of united front we were going to present to the CAB.

"Of course, the Civil Aeronautics Administration and the CAB people were excluded from that meeting; we didn't bother to invite them. Somebody had a few bottles up there and the meeting got going off in a grand and glorious style, and everybody immediately became an orator.

"They'd jump up on their chair and they'd talk till everybody yelled, 'Sit down!' or 'Shut up!' and then someone else would take the floor, and that went on until — oh, I guess daylight the next morning. And then everybody went to bed.

"Well, the hearings were to start at 9 A.M. and there wasn't anybody there. At least not enough for a meeting. I was there, and Noel Wien and one or two others, but nobody else made it.

"Here the place was packed with townspeople, and the CAB and CAA people were all ready to start explaining the law to us, but there was nobody there to hear it.

"They wanted to know what happened. Finally someone said, 'Well, they had a party last night and I think maybe they're kinda late this morning.' So they postponed the meeting until two o'clock in the afternoon.

"So those of us that were there and able to get around went to wake the others up. Some of them had gone to bed at the Anchorage Hotel, and since it was August, it was a warm night. But someone had turned up the steam heat and the windows were all shut tight, and all of them were passed out and almost dead for want of a little fresh air.

"After we got the windows open and they commenced to revive, they either got sick or hungry, and some of them both.

"About noon they were getting in pretty good shape and the meeting started off at two o'clock and went right on through without any interruptions."

The CAB had a team there: Raymond Stowe, who was the

hearing examiner, and an attorney and so forth. The first airline to be heard was Cordova Air Service. No one really knew what to expect, and Smitty said that there was this big crowd of people to hear him stumble around and testify in front of them.

The Civil Aeronautics Act of 1938 was landmark legislation; it called for establishment of a good, dependable air transportation system, for building up the economy of Alaska through such service, for navigation aids, airports, setting of safety standards and schedules, payment of subsidies to make sure the standards and the schedules were kept, and the stabilization of fares.

The law was specific about including Alaska. At that time most legislation specifically *excluded* Alaska, leaving the northern territory without the assistance that aided the economic build-up of other states.

With the setting of subsidies was to come auditing of the airlines' books, so that there would be no abuse of the payments. When the auditor went over Cordova Air Service's books, he told Smitty jokingly, "Why, you've been broke for ten years!"

The matter of fare stabilization was more than it might seem today. In the charter business going on in Alaska, one passenger might pay five dollars for a trip while another paid fifty. Most planes in those days hauled perhaps five passengers, and sometimes no two persons paid the same fare. The pilot just made deals until he had gathered what he needed to make the flight.

After the act went into effect that practice ceased because, as Smitty explained, "You had to file a tariff, and if that wasn't a chore! Who in hell knew what a tariff was? But we got a lot of help from Tom Donohue and the government. They had people in here to guide us on that.

"But it took a lot of guts to turn down a guy that came along and said I only got twenty dollars and I'd sure like to go along (on a trip that was set at thirty dollars). But they watched that real close, and if you'd taken their money you were violating your tariff, and they were trying to catch somebody doing it to make a few horrible examples so people would know they meant business.

"But it turned out better for the public in the long run because — well, maybe you lost money on some trips, but with the federal criteria and method of paying you a subsidy, they picked up the loss.

"They paid on an annual basis. What you'd have was a mail rate hearing, and they'd determine how much you lost that year and how much you'd need for subsidy and how much your investment was, and they'd pay you on your investment. And they had their auditors going over your books constantly to keep you honest.

"So we never got by with anything, but it put us on a sound financial basis. By having the government behind us that way, we could go to the banks and borrow money to buy newer airplanes. We could pay our help a little more — at least we could pay them regularly — and we could fix up our facilities."

Safety standards improved, too. The airlines had been of necessity running their planes until they were almost falling apart, but after the act they could afford to have the proper maintenance on them.

Despite the difficulties, aviation was growing in Alaska far more rapidly than in other parts of the United States due mainly to the lack of ground transportation. The CAA reported that Alaska planes were providing enough mail service for Alaska's 60,000 residents to equal the service provided 2,880,000 residents in the states, as much passenger service as for a district of 1,380,000 persons, and enough freight and express as for 62,040,000. It only seemed natural that Alaska was entitled to a big share of the dollar spent for air navigation aids, for airfields and for air mail service.

The Civil Aeronautics Act of 1938 was to bring about many of these improvements, and to accomplish them rather rapidly. But at the time of the hearings in Alaska, little was known of the eventual ramifications. While Smitty was testifying before the CAB in Anchorage, he was unaware of the eventual importance of what was happening. His simple answer to a simple question that day was to cost him thousands of dollars.

Those long, miserable flights to Southeastern Alaska during the summer of 1938, and the flights to Juneau, Wrangell and Petersburg, fell within what was known as the "Grandfather Period." Stowe asked Smitty if he wanted the route to Juneau from Cordova. Smitty, still thinking like a pilot rather than a manager, could only remember what a tough route it was. He recalled all the trips up and down the ladder at Yakutat, fueling the plane, and the fog and short gas supply, so he said, "No." He spent much money later to get the very route he could have had that day for simply saying "Yes."

They were all learning as they went along with the Civil Aeronautics Act of 1938.

One thing Smitty remembers very clearly is that during the hearings, the news came through that Germany had attacked Poland, and soon the British and French got into the fight, and it was evident to everybody that we were going to have another world war.

What the CAB started in the way of airport building and navigation aids now became imperative through the threat of war.

After the Anchorage hearings, the CAB moved to Fairbanks, Juneau, Nome and back to Fairbanks to finish up. There were thirty-six applications for routes, and the CAB made its recommendations from those and the testimony at the hearings. They finished in October.

They didn't quit there. Soon they brought their own plane to Alaska to begin building navigation aids. Within a year they started to construct airports.

In March of 1940, Bertha gave birth to their first son, Kenneth. He was due on March 24, Easter Sunday. Bertha had spotted a small item in the newspaper, which said, "In 1940 Easter fell on March 24. Since the introduction of the Gregorian calendar in 1582, Easter has fallen on March 24 just once before, in 1799. There will not be another Easter on March 24 until the year 2391."

Bertha went into labor on Easter Sunday, but the baby was not born until the next day.

In August of 1941 the CAB was back again to take more testimony, and Smitty again appeared before that body. There was a lot of bush flying to canneries and mining camps. How best to serve these clients and still bring order to the airline business was the big concern. Smitty testified that he felt the best way to accomplish this would be to allow freedom to fly almost anywhere on any type of charter, but to confine the companies to a certain base where their hangars and repair shops were located. This, he felt, would tend to restrict their radius of operation and at the same time give them freedom to meet the needs within their own area. The concept of small airline exclusive areas had come out of the 1939 hearings; this was just a refinement of the idea.

In September 1941, while flying a routine mail run on Prince William Sound, Mudhole Smith spotted a Japanese submarine in the Montague Island area. Smitty saw the slim black outline of the sub and started to circle it.

As soon as the sub spotted Smitty's plane, it dived. Smitty realized it must be a Japanese sub, but inasmuch as the country was not at war, he didn't mention it to anyone until next morning in the Alaska Communications System office.

The operator took it a bit more seriously. He sent a telegram reporting the incident. Within a few days a representative of the

U.S. Navy appeared, looking for Mudhole Smith. Smitty recounted the story of seeing the sub in Drier Bay, and was told that an Alaska Steamship Company ship had sighted the same sub about 3 P.M. that same day. It was going out the lower end of Prince William Sound, near Latouche, headed for the open waters of the Gulf of Alaska.

War was definitely in the air. Alaskans had been warning the State Department for years that the Japanese fishing fleets in the Aleutians were up to more than pirating salmon. They had been scouting the mostly uncharted islands and mapping them; for what, no one could say.

By 1941, airports were under construction all around Alaska. It was not clear whether they were a peacetime effort aimed at better transportation or another harbinger of war.

The airport at Mile 13, out of Cordova, was built in 1941. The Morrison-Knudsen Company had the contract to put in the CAA (now Federal Aeronautics Administration) weather station. Until then, Cordova's airport was still the small strip carved out of the mountainside at Eyak Lake.

The new CAA construction was served by a small rail line run over the tracks of the former Copper River & Northwestern Railway and dubbed the "CivAir Short Line," but this method of getting back and forth was not too satisfactory to the "Brass Hats" on the Mile 13 construction job. They had a small strip built on the duck flats at Mile 13 so they could travel faster. The Morrison-Knudsen Company had contracts to build a series of airfields and FAA stations, and they flew the circuit frequently, staying only a few hours in each place. When the first pioneer strip was done, they chartered Smitty to fly out and land on it to see what he thought of it. Smitty did, and reported it to be a fine little field. So he was the first pilot to land on the new Mile 13 airport. He would be, the next year, the first to land on the new Eielson AFB field in Fairbanks, too.

Another couple of airports under construction during 1941 and 1942 were at Cape Yakataga, where Smitty had been caught in the surf in the bearskin flying suit, and at Yakutat a hundred miles farther down the coast, where he had toted gas cans down the ladder to pour in the tank through a funnel. At the same time, the new harbor and rail line from Whittier were under construction.

During the months bracketing Pearl Harbor, there was a great deal of activity, some of it civilian, some military, some a little of both. The building of airports and the supplying of soldiers and civilian construction workers became a big problem. Alaska was for all intents and purposes a huge island: everything had to be shipped in. Until airplanes could be pressed into such service, all of it came by ship. Alaska produced little in the way of provisions, and Alaskans traditionally purchased a full year's supplies at a time. Thus the resident population had ample provisions but not enough for the newly superimposed group of workers and troops.

Early in 1942 Colonel Talley, who was in charge of a group of six Army colonels, came to Cordova by ship with the idea of flying to Yakutat. He chartered Smitty to make the flight in the Travel Air.

"When I took them down there, the only information I had was that there was a strip to land on at Yakutat, but when I got there the strip was a road! The officer in command had built a good road for about two thousand feet, and it made an excellent landing strip. The commander told me afterward that mine was the first airplane to land there."

Smitty and many other bush pilots were adding to their string of first landings at the new airports all over the territory.

Smitty found the Yakutat airport was in desperate need of supplies that Mudhole knew were available in Cordova. While he was waiting for Colonel Talley to complete his business, Smitty chartered his plane to the officer in charge (with Talley's okay) to fly to Cordova and pick up a load.

It was Sunday, but Smitty didn't think he'd have any trouble getting the supplies. A man was sent along to take care of the paper work. In Cordova Smitty rousted out some employees of the Cordova Commercial Company and a few other merchants in town, and they filled the airplane.

When he arrived at Yakutat, he found he still had plenty of time so they flew back for another load. The same fellow was along with a new list and they went through the whole thing again.

It was late in the day when Smitty flew Colonel Talley and his group back to Cordova. It was one of the most profitable days that Cordova Air Service had ever had. The Travel Air charge was forty-five dollars an hour, the going rate at the time, and each round trip was four hours.

The airfields begun in 1941 before the outbreak of war were better built than those after Pearl Harbor, when things looked pretty critical and many corners were cut. The airfields were built by excavating the tundra, refilling with gravel and then laying the strip on top. Cordova's Mile 13 airstrip, having been one of the first, was excavated a full eighteen feet and back-filled, and after all these years of use, it has not broken up. Some built later were excavated only a few feet and had to be done over again after the war.

When the bombs rained on Pearl Harbor, Alaska was caught as flat-footed as everyone else, but it was more real to Alaskans because they were so much closer to Japan.

In the wake of Pearl Harbor, of course, came the rapid loss of Guam, Indochina, Thailand, Wake, Hong Kong, Singapore, Malaya, Java, and Burma. Australia was a heartbeat away. By May 1942, less than six months after Pearl Harbor, the Philippines fell.

In June 1942, concurrently with the Battle of Midway, the war came to Alaska. The Japanese bombed Dutch Harbor, and shortly afterward they invaded Attu and Kiska, and dug in with their troops on American soil for the first time.

Because Seward was the only port for the Alaska Railroad, even before the war started the Army was worried about its vulnerability. They built Whittier at the head of Passage Canal as a second port. It was connected to Turnagain Arm through Portage Pass by means of two long tunnels, one of them over five-and-a-half miles long.

Whittier was begun in 1941. Sheldon Simmons, a pilot from Southeast Alaska, flew the tunnel contractor to Whittier from Juneau. The *Cordova Times* commented on the flight: "The spectacular feature of the trip was that the contractor reached Cordova from New York 26½ hours later by the clock. The flight was acutally made in 31½ hours, discounting the time gained in flying westward with the sun." Such speed was considered incredible.

War!

When the war broke out, the bush pilots offered their services to General Buckner for the defense of Alaska, but they were told they were not wanted in the Army. What they were doing was exactly what was needed. Between the Morrison-Knudsen Company and the Army Engineers, all sorts of projects were under way at the same time and Morrison-Knudsen was hiring all the experienced bush pilots they could get.

Beside Cape Yakataga, airports were built at Gustavus (at the entrance to Glacier Bay), Northway (near the Yukon border), along the Kuskokwim River at McGrath, Bethel and Aniak, and King Salmon. Taken together, the projects made a huge circle. Inspectors from Morrison-Knudsen flew this circle, inspecting the jobs. They stayed overnight at a camp, then flew on the next day, until they made the whole circuit and began another round. Material was delivered to the projects in the same way.

Along about the middle of 1942, Smitty quit Cordova Air Service and went to work for Morrison-Knudsen and Harold Gillam. Bertha and Kenneth were in Nebraska and intended to stay there till the war was over.

Harold Gillam, who had become chief pilot for Morrison-Knudsen, flew to Cordova and contacted Smitty with a job offer. The two fliers went to the Model Cafe in Cordova to talk. What Morrison-Knudsen had in mind was opening up the new Northway airfield and flying freight in from Nabesna, which was at the end of the highway out of Valdez. (The Alaska Highway had not yet been built, of course.) It would be a sixty-mile hop with a Boeing 80-A.

The airport at Northway had high priority with the military, because they were trying to send supplies to the Russians. They were ferrying planes via Nome to Siberia, but the distance between Whitehorse and Fairbanks, the next airport, was just a bit too far. An airport about halfway between, with a good range station, was what they needed. A number of planes had been lost because they ran out of fuel on that long hop.

Mudhole Smith began flying freight to Northway about May 1st. The airport was paved and the range station installed and working by the 28th of August.

Smitty flew one of two planes, each of which had two crews so both planes were flying twenty-four hours a day, carrying about six thousand pounds each trip. Smitty kept track of the tonnage he flew that summer, and it came to more than seventy-six hundred tons.

The airport at Northway was completed ahead of schedule. In the latter part of October, Smitty flew in a load of food.

"It was getting dark when I landed at Northway. They had a bed for me and I was dead tired, so I went right to sleep. I was right alongside the runway but aircraft noise didn't wake me because I lived with it.

"When I woke up the next morning and walked outside, there were twenty-one DC3s on that airport. They had landed there throughout the night because Fairbanks was socked in.

"I had never seen so many DC3s in one bunch — In spite of the night landings, only one of them had run off the end of the field. It had gone out into the stumps and they'd squeezed the landing gear together and stopped the plane. No other damage.

"All summer long, any time you stood on that airport you could hear one airplane right above, one fading out in the distance toward Fairbanks, and another coming up from Whitehorse. I think it was that way all twenty-four hours of the day; one, I'd say, every fifteen or twenty minutes. You'd see DC3s with Delta Airlines signs on them and Eastern Airlines and all the rest. They'd taken them off the scheduled routes, loaded them up with men or freight and headed them north to Nome or Fairbanks. Some went on across to Siberia.

"Between Fairbanks and Nome lay another huge stretch with few airfields. They started immediately building one at Galena and finished it pretty fast. All the bush pilots used Ruby, that was a favorite stop. In the wintertime, of course, everybody operated on skis, and you could land anyplace, almost, on the Yukon River. But by the end of 1942 there were fields at Moses Point, Tanana, and at Nenana, too."

Smitty made the first landing on the airport at Eielson AFB in Fairbanks. He says, "Of course it wasn't official but it was still the first one. Morrison-Knudsen had two loads of men to take there late in the afternoon. On the daylight trip I landed on what is now a very small portion of the runway.

"On the second trip it was pitch dark when we got there. On each side of the tiny strip were tents where the construction workers lived. I thought the lights from the tents would show up and make good landing markers, but it was late enough when I arrived that most of the lights were out. The guys had gone to bed.

"I thought I knew where the strip was, though. So I put the gear and flaps down, and the landing lights on. They showed I wasn't on the strip — I was to one side of the runway and I was going to plow right along a line of tents!

"I opened the motor wide and told the mechanic, who was in the co-pilot's seat, to pull up the gear. He made a mistake and pulled up the flaps. We settled lower and I had to shove the throttle wide open.

"The plane had a thousand-horsepower engine. We pulled on out, and got the gear up. I made a circle, and — boy! when I came around again, I had plenty of lights down there. I had no trouble landing.

The Travel Air was a popular plane among Alaska bush pilots. One of Art Woodley's Travel Airs is shown as it was before Mudhole became a "multiple ace." Smith was landing the Yellow Peril, *but the plane's brakes were unable to stop it before it plowed into three of Woodley's Travel Airs.*

"I couldn't have been more than five feet above those tents and all the guys sound asleep in them. I'll bet they never before had had such an effective wake-up call."

The Boeing 80-A was the plane flown most often by Smitty during this period. Morrison-Knudsen had two of them, large airplanes for the time, with three engines. The 80-A was a good plane, except for one flaw: It had mechanical brakes, and "it took forever to stop it," Smitty recalled. The pilots dubbed it the *"Yellow Peril."*

One of the favorite nicknames going the rounds was "Chinese Ace,"* a title won by anyone who wrecked a plane on the ground.

---

*The name came from a story told of training pilots in China. The Chinese pilots were bright young men, but they didn't speak English. The trainers were bright young Englishmen who didn't speak Chinese.

The squadron of pilots was about to solo. The trainer told them (through an interpreter), "When you land, keep your nose up!" So the first Chinese lad took off, made his solo, and on landing kept his nose so high that he wrecked four planes on the ground. So anyone who wrecked a plane on the ground became known as a "Chinese Ace."

One very cold day Smitty was taking off in the 80-A with a load of boiler tubes and brass, when the left engine quit. The plane was halfway down the runway and started to veer to the right. Smitty poured power on the right engine to turn it away from the hangars and airplanes on the edge of the runway. The carburetor heat was inadequate for the extremely cold weather and the right engine also coughed and died. That left him with only one engine running.

The plane was headed for Woodley Airways hangar and the brakes just wouldn't stop it. He plowed into three of Art Woodley's Travel Air 6000s, one of them loaded with passengers and pilot Jack Wildworth. The Boeing then swung around to the left and went through the side of Woodley's hangar, to the astonishment of a mechanic at his workbench who found himself looking up at the nose engine. Fortunately, no one was hurt.

From then on, Mudhole took a lot of ribbing for being a multiple Chinese Ace.

This same airplane, outfitted with hydraulic brakes a few years later, was to prove extremely useful to Mudhole.

Kuskokwim Mail Run

In October of 1942, Harold Gillam approached Mudhole with a proposition.

"How would you like to fly the winter mail run along the Kuskokwim River?"

Although Gillam was chief pilot for the Morrison-Knudsen Company, Gillam Airways still had the contract for the mail delivery to the dozen or more villages along that five-hundred-mile stretch of river.

"I thought you sold all your Pilgrims to Morrison-Knudsen at the beginning of the war."

"I did, but I still have one for the mail contract. The job pays $850 a month, and you'll still remain on the Morrison-Knudsen payroll so you won't lose any seniority."

They discussed the proposal for awhile, and Smitty thought it was a pretty good deal. It involved one round trip a week, starting from Fairbanks on Thursday, with overnight stops at McGrath and Bethel, and McGrath again on the way back to Fairbanks.

There were a lot of stops on the route, only two of them between Fairbanks and McGrath. They were Minchumina and

Medfra. But on the next day's flight from McGrath to Bethel, there were eight or ten villages where he would have to put down with mail, freight and passengers. The flight would take all day, especially with the short winter days to come.

"You'll be on wheels yet," Gillam explained, "and will have to land on sand bars in the river at most of the villages. Later on, when the river is frozen solid, we'll put you on skis.

"I've got a person to meet you at every stop to help load and unload. That will save time for you and your flight mechanic, so you can get done before dark."

Mudhole went to Fairbanks in early November, arriving on a Tuesday evening. He spent most of Wednesday studying the map and talking to the flight mechanic who had flown the route the year before with Gillam. Mudhole had never flown the Kuskokwim so he had a lot of work familiarizing himself with the local terrain and landmarks, but with the mechanic's help, the pilot felt he had himself fairly well oriented for the trip.

Dawn broke gray and threatening, but the winds were calm as Mudhole warmed up the Pilgrim, a single-engine craft. It carried nine passengers, plus the pilot and flight engineer and a good load of freight.

Two uneventful hours later he put down on the sand bar near Minchumina, unloaded the freight and two passengers, loaded two passengers and some more freight and took off for Medfra, the second and last stop on the way to McGrath.

Soon after takeoff he ran into snow. Telida Mountain was somewhere nearby and he was flying through the foothills of the Alaska Range to the north. From his map studies of the day before, he knew there was an old dog sled trail running from McGrath to Fairbanks, and peering through the window he soon picked it up. It wound hither and yon, and sometimes he'd lose it only to find it a few miles farther on. It was known as a good compass trail.

As the snow increased, visibility became poorer and poorer. Smitty tried to call up a photo memory of the map and searched for landmarks directing him to Medfra. Snowflakes fell in tiny round globules that stuck momentarily to the windshield, then moved with the force of the wind to one side and away, leaving tiny wet tracks that further obscured his vision. Smitty noted with satisfaction that the snow was light and fluffy and blew off the wings and side windows without sticking, which meant there was no icing. The country was heavily wooded, too, and there was no danger of a whiteout.

Visibility continued to deteriorate and soon it became a heavy snow squall. He could see an eighth of a mile or less.

"Too dangerous to fly in these foothills now," he thought, altering course to the left to come out over the flatlands. There was less hazard but he no longer had the dog sled trail to follow.

With the alteration in course and so little visibility, he doubted he could find Medfra. He selected a compass course, hoping that he was headed for McGrath. Occasionally a small hill would appear through the thick swirling snow. He continually had to alter course to go around them, then try to pick up his compass heading on the other side. After what seemed an hour of such dodging, he was not sure where he was or where he was going.

Mudhole knew McGrath had a range station, but his fuel supply was getting low. He was equipped with two sixty-five gallon tanks and the last of these was nearly empty. Then only a twenty-gallon reserve tank remained.

Smitty turned on the radio to pick up the range station at McGrath. He knew nothing about instrument flying except that the range station sent out a series of Morse Code signals: dot-dash for an "A" signal, and dash-dot for an "N" signal. Where the two overlapped he could hear a solid beep, meaning he was on course. In his detours around hills, sometimes he'd pick up the "A" and sometimes the "N" and finally the beep between them. The signals kept getting louder, which was reassuring.

Still, would his fuel supply hold out or would he have to put down on one of the small lakes he could see below? If so, would the ice hold the heavily loaded Pilgrim?

Suddenly the motor quit. His last sixty-five gallon tank was dry. He quickly switched to the twenty-gallon reserve. The motor sputtered back to life and he flew on, no more than a hundred feet off the ground.

Below him the brush and trees showed up as black in the white world of snow, but it was an endlessly confusing black pattern with no detail to show where he was. Only the dot-dash or dash-dot of the "A" and "N" signals telling him McGrath was out there somewhere ahead.

He glanced at the fuel gauge. The twenty-gallon spare tank's needle hovered perilously close to zero.

All at once he spotted something below. He leaned close to the window. He could see the white-black edges of a river, with jagged cakes of ice running thick.

"Ah, the Kuskokwim," Smitty sighed. He knew it ran through

McGrath, so he locked onto the river. The needle on the reserve tank was now down to zero.

Suddenly out of the white mist loomed the five FAA towers of the McGrath range station. As he dodged the towers, he came over the village and the runway, which was McGrath's main street. He made a steep bank and went to land. His speed was so great he almost ran off the end of the runway, into the river. He stopped ten feet short.

When he later filled the 20-gallon reserve tank, it took 19.8 gallons.

Smitty and the nine passengers deplaned and went into the store for pie and coffee while the plane was unloaded. The passengers, who were well acquainted in the area, shopped at the Northern Commercial Company store or looked up friends in town.

Since Morrison-Knudsen boarded crews in McGrath, Smitty spent a restful night before starting off the next morning for Bethel and the many stops in between.

At 8 A.M. the weather was much improved and Mudhole took off with his full load. His first stop was to be Stony River, but after looking it over he saw only a very small sand bar and decided to pass it up. Next stop was Sleetmute, which he made, and on to Crooked Creek. The bar at Crooked Creek was smooth and about two miles long. The river was frozen and he was met by a young woman with a dog sled. She came up the riverbank and crossed on the ice to where the Pilgrim was taxiing to a stop.

She became one of Smitty's favorite contacts, for she was always there on time. She'd stay and wait patiently if he was late, regardless of the weather or temperature, and if he was forced to move on, she'd be there the next day to meet him. She was known to him as the "limo driver."

The last stop he was able to make was Aniak. Shortly after taking off from Aniak, a freezing drizzle began. The Pilgrim grew heavy as ice kept building on the surfaces of the airplane. Ice on the windshield cut visibility almost to zero. Mudhole stayed close to the river, making every turn the crooked river did. The wings were slow about coming back up from each bank. He could see the ice forming on them, and the motor was running rough, which indicated that the prop blades were picking up ice also. He headed for Bethel, flying barely ten feet above the river ice, and arrived with no serious consequences.

He spent the night there and about 4 A.M. the next day loaded the mail and freight. Then he and the flight mechanic worked on the wings, which were coated with freezing drizzle. The passengers helped when they could, and at other times stood around stamping their feet, huddled in little groups trying to keep warm. Flying as a passenger tended to be uncomfortable. Waiting rooms were virtually unknown even in "airports." People practiced patience because it still beat the alternative — dog-sled travel.

While working on the wings, Smitty slipped and poked his elbow through the fabric. There was a further delay while they froze a patch over the hole. Then they put covers over the wings again and worked underneath them to knock off the ice.

It was afternoon before the job was finished. In a freezing drizzle Smitty took off for the return trip. The drizzle changed to blinding snow near Aniak, and got progressively worse. The last stop he could make before dark was Napamiute, where he decided they would stop for the night because it was just too dangerous to go on in the dark and the snow.

As they landed on the sand bar, a couple of young men came across the river in a boat. Farther up the river at Crooked Creek it was frozen over, but here it was still running full of ice floes.

Smitty and his passengers got into the small boat. He knew the boys had handled boats on the river all their lives and were experts, but they had their hands full trying to keep from being capsized by the huge ice cakes pushed along by the current.

Mudhole was used to the air, but this was something different. If they capsized there was no hope in the chill waters of the Kuskokwim. "I sure had some squeamish feelings," he said afterward. Of all the close calls he had over the years, Mudhole still remembers that boat crossing as one of the most harrowing trips of his life.

The hospitality at Napamiute was good, with a comfortable roadhouse, good food and a warm bed. Next morning the weather was fair. Smitty went on to McGrath with no problems, making all his stops including Stony River, which he had missed on the way downriver.

At McGrath there was still daylight left. Being a day late due to his stop at Napaimute, he decided to go as far as possible before nightfall.

His next stop was Medfra, another place he had failed to land on the trip down. While he was unloading the mail, the man who met him said, "Boy, I was sure disappointed you didn't land the other day when you came over."

Smitty was startled. "Over? I didn't come over here."

"No, you were just east of here a little way, because your motor stopped right out there and I could hear it just as plain."

So Smitty knew he had been almost to Medfra when he switched to his spare twenty-gallon tank. He was closer on course than he had realized.

"I really learned a good lesson on that trip down the river from Medfra to McGrath," he said.

The next day he was back in Fairbanks, a day late on his first trip. It was the only trip he failed to complete on the daily schedule.

"They had some of the coldest weather I had ever been in," he recalled. "Several mornings we took off from McGrath when it was sixty-five degrees below zero, and maybe a degree or two colder than that. It was always around sixty degrees below. We didn't shut down on account of the temperature. We just fire-potted the engine, and got the oil good and hot before pouring it in. Then we yanked off the wing and engine covers, threw them into the cabin and away we went."

With the winter days, the trips took from sun-up to long past dark. The weather was normally lousy, but the part from Aniak to Bethel was the hardest part of the trip.

Smitty had plenty of chance to reflect on Gillam's advice about ignoring the "point of no return." He landed at Minchumina, the last stop on his way home, and took off on a compass course for Nenana. He was in the air about five minutes before it began snowing. He'd turn on the landing lights, and all he could see was thick whirling white flakes. He took out a flashlight and shone it on the wings. The snow wasn't sticking.

"No ice," he thought, but the wings were thick with snow. "Maybe I'd better go back and land at Minchumina."

He made a 180 degree turn, plotted a reciprocal course on his compass and headed towards the place he had just left.

He could see nothing at all and began to worry. "What if I miss Lake Minchumina? There are no lights there, and I don't know the country very well."

So he changed his mind, turned around once more and headed for Fairbanks again.

He turned on his landing lights occasionally, and aimed the flashlight at the wings. It was easier to fly at night in the snow than in the daytime, because in the daylight the swirling flakes created a hypnotic effect.

He could make out little lakes and potholes as he flew over. Halfway between Minchumina and Nenana, he remembered there was a little hill. About the time his watch said he should be halfway between Minchumina and Nenana, he spotted the hill. Another hurdle passed.

He was probably bucking a stiff headwind without knowing it. Time stretched on and on, and where was Nenana?

Then he saw a little flicker of light. He burst into a clear spot and below him were the lights of Nenana. Ahead of him from Nenana to Fairbanks stretched the broad "highway" of the Tanana River, a frozen white trail, easy to follow.

There were field lights at Fairbanks, something still rare in Alaska. He landed and went into the hangar. Everyone was surprised to see him. The bookkeeper and two mechanics at Gillam's had checked with Minchumina, asking if Smitty had been there, and the answer was, "Yeah. A long time ago." His time of departure had the men at the hangar worried, and they were even preparing another airplane for the mail run if he didn't make it.

Frank Bligh, an old pilot who had flown Pilgrims many times had told them, "He just ain't had the time to get here. Give him another ten minutes." About ten minutes later they heard the Pilgrim approaching.

Smitty wondered what might have become of him if he had persisted in trying to find Minchumina in the dark and the snow. He decided there was such a thing as playing it too safe.

"After that when I started for a destination, and had everything figured out, I never again turned around anyplace on the Kuskokwim."

Railroad to Nome

In January of 1943, Gillam pulled Smitty off the mail run and sent him to Nome where the Army was in the process of surveying a railway to connect the Alaska Railroad with Nome.

At the time the Germans were invading Russia, and their blitz was a real threat to Moscow. If Moscow fell, the Russians would have to retreat to Siberia, taking the seat of government with them. Then the Nome railroad connection would be absolutely vital for the survival of Russia, by providing a dependable supply line through Nome, and Teller farther up the coast.

Mudhole's first job was to fly diesel oil to the survey "train,"

"Thrill 'em, Spill 'em, Never Kill 'em Gillam." Pioneer pilot Harold Gillam set the standard for Mudhole and other Alaska pilots and created a legend for himself as the pilot who always made it through to destination. Fate eventually caught up with Gillam, and in January, 1943, he was reported missing on a flight from Ketchikan. It was later discovered that he had died walking for help for the passengers who remained in his plane.

Caterpillars pulling wanigans. A wanigan is a small cabin on skids, providing quarters for the men to sleep and eat in. The survey trains had run out of diesel, used not only to run the Cats, but also to heat the quarters and cook.

"When I arrived in Nome, I reported to the Army Engineers, who immediately started me hauling oil to the survey trains. I could take six barrels in the Pilgrim. I landed on the frozen tundra near the trains, which were all stopped, just lying there dead. In two days I had them running.

"Then they got some Northwest Airlines pilots with Nordyne Norsemans to take over the oil hauling. I was assigned to fly up and down the Arctic Coast buying dog feed. They had thirty-five hundred dogs pulling sleds on the survey operation between Nulato and the head of Norton Sound. That took a lot of dog food.

"The closest you could land was Nulato on one end and Norton Sound on the other. But we would find a stream or river where a Pilgrim could be landed for unloading, and that shortened the distance considerably The dogs would come there and pick up a barrel of diesel oil and haul it back.

"It was a day's trip from where their survey party was, and a day's trip going back with the barrel, so it gives you an idea how many dogs there were working all the time.

"My job was to go up and down the Arctic coast, to Unalakleet and Hamilton and all those towns, and buy all the dog food I could, and fly it to one of the landing places for them to pick up.

"They gave me a book of vouchers, and I would go into a trader's store and tell him that I was there to buy all the dog food I could get. I could haul about twenty-five hundred pounds in the Pilgrim, and I had a flight mechanic who helped me load and unload. The trader would pass the word around the village, and in a few minutes the sled loads started coming in. I left the voucher with the trader, who sent it in for pay. He in turn paid the people who supplied the dog food — or extended their credit for what they bought at his store, so I guess it boosted the economy along the coast.

"After a few days of handling all that blubber, dried salmon, the entrails of whales and everything the dogs would eat, you smelled like your cargo. It was all frozen, of course, but it still rubbed off and came to life when you got in by the fire and warmed up.

"I had to make one trip a week into Fairbanks, to pick up a load of meat to fly into the engineers' camp at Nome. At Fairbanks I got a chance to take a bath and put on clean clothes, but between times everybody would walk circles around me. They didn't want to get too close, especially downwind.

"In Nome we had a room at the Wallace Hotel, which had hot and cold running water most of the time, but the restaurants sometimes closed for want of something to cook. The only steaks were reindeer, and I got so tired of them I don't think I've eaten one since.

"I ate at the Army Engineers' mess at first — they were the people I was working for — but one day the colonel barred all civilians. All the restaurants were closed at the time, for about two weeks. It left us to go to the grocery store, and we'd buy cans of beans and sardines and whatever we could get and try to warm them on the steam radiators in the hotel room. That's pretty tough at forty degrees below, coffee or tea never got very warm on those radiators. When we went to Fairbanks we'd always time it so we could stay overnight in Nulato. The trader there had nice clean beds and his young daughters could really cook. We had some of the best food that I've ever eaten at Nulato.

"In the morning we'd get up and have hot cakes, bacon and eggs, and ham and everything. And above all, we had three or four cups of good hot coffee that would tide us for the day."

In January, 1943, word came that Harold Gillam was missing. Smitty heard it from his old friend Jack Jefford, who was now with the CAA. Jack flew into Nome from Anchorage and told Smitty that Gillam had been missing from out of Ketchikan for about two weeks.

The next morning Mudhole Smith got in his plane and left Nome. "I didn't say goodbye, yes or no, to anybody. I just took my flight mechanic and we filled her up with gas and took off for Anchorage. I got into Anchorage late that night and they wanted to know what I was doing there. I told them I had heard that Harold was missing and I came down to get in on the search. The motor in the Pilgrim was not running good and after they listened to it they decided they'd better do some major work on it.

"I tried to get another airplane to fly to Ketchikan so I could join the search but there just was nothing available. Gillam was found a couple of weeks later, dead. He died walking out for help for his passengers, who were left with the airplane."

There were airplanes in Anchorage, and they started Smitty flying right away. Now that he was based in Anchorage, he sent for Bertha, and she returned from Nebraska.

The Morrison-Knudsen Company sent Smitty on some flights down to Chirikof and Sanak islands in the Aleutians. The company had built most of the airfields in Alaska with the exception of those on the Aleutian Chain. They did have the contract for the one at Cold Bay. "Slim" DeLong, who had been a superintendent with Morrison-Knudsen, went into the Army Engineers as a full colonel, and Smitty and the Morrison-Knudsen pilots did a lot of flying for the outfit that DeLong commanded. Beyond Cold Bay lay the war zone, so civilian pilots seldom went far down the Chain, because as Smitty said, "the Army didn't want civilians messing around in a war zone." The Japanese were on Kiska, and they'd already bombed Dutch Harbor.

Smitty flew to Sanak Island, between Dutch Harbor and Cold Bay, on the gulf side of the Aleutians. There was no airfield there so the plane he flew was an amphibian Grumman Goose.

"We flew to Chirikof Island, then across to Sanak Island, a long way with a heavily loaded airplane. That's the roughest piece of water in the world, I think. On Chirikof we'd land on the beach. On Sanak we'd land in the bay.

"On Sanak Island there was a homesteader who raised cattle. Meat was rationed, so Morrison-Knudsen made a deal with the rancher for his surplus cattle. They'd butcher them and we'd fly the beef to Anchorage for their camps. Some of it was pretty tough, because the cattle had been around for quite a while, but some of it was pretty good, too. It was really a Godsend to the rancher, he didn't have to worry about transporting it out. I thought it was a Godsend, too, because I'd see that I got a few T-bones off of those shipments."

The Yellow Peril Rides Again

In 1944 the Aleutians were free of Japanese troops. Most of the airfields that the Morrison-Knudsen Company had contracted to build were finished and no new projects were being started.

"My job was winding down," Smitty said. "The need for pilots and mechanics was not very great, and they were letting people go. At least, whenever anyone quit, they never replaced him.

"Then, to cap things off, Morrison-Knudsen had a big hangar fire in Anchorage, and most of the planes in it were destroyed. Although they rebuilt the hangar, they still had a surplus of pilots, and it was obviously time to start looking around for something else."

Something else did show up. Word came through that the Civil Aeronautics Board had denied the 1943 merger of Cordova Air Service with a new firm, the Alaska Star Airlines. The two airlines would have to return to their original status as two separate carriers, and the money received by Cordova Air Service stockholders, thirty thousand dollars, had to be repaid.

The stockholders of Cordova Air Service asked Mudhole Smith

to come to Cordova and discuss the future of the airline. He was still a stockholder himself and interested in its survival. The other stockholders, most of whom had been in Cordova for the duration of the war, had watched with dismay while the air service declined.

Especially alarming was the deterioration in the bush service that had been the mainstay of Cordova Air. The management of the new airline had moved headquarters to Anchorage, leaving only a token service behind. It was down to one airplane and one pilot, and they'd call him to Anchorage at times for two weeks to a month. Naturally Cordova residents were very dissatisfied.

Mudhole was still working for Morrison-Knudsen though there was little left to do. He made a number of trips back and forth between Anchorage and Cordova, sizing things up and negotiating. He heard disquieting rumors about conditions in some of the bush communities and mining camps that had been good customers of Cordova Air Service and who had no other way to get supplies. Some of the points he had serviced in the Copper and Tanana river valleys had not seen an airplane for months.

He borrowed one of Morrison-Knudsen's smaller planes and flew up there. What he found confirmed the worst of the stories. Chisana, especially, was in a bad way. The old miners had not had an airplane for eight months — no food, no supplies, no mail, no news.

The only way out of Chisana was either on foot through Cooper Pass or Skolai Pass. None of the miners at Chisana were under sixty-five, and some of them were over seventy years old.

They had held a meeting shortly before Smitty landed to decide what they were going to do. Their supplies were so short that if nothing happened within two days, they would start to walk out. They didn't know if they could make it, considering their age, but they knew they had to try or starve when winter came.

Smitty's airplane was truly a welcome sight when it came winging in. One of the miners showed Smitty his flour barrel, and although he had scraped it down carefully, it had yielded only two cups of flour.

Mudhole had picked up their mail, which had collected at Chitina, and they tore open the letters with eager hands. As for news, they now had a chance to read the newspapers and find out all that had happened in the war during the past eight months.

Smitty took down their orders for everything they needed and left for Anchorage to return the Morrison-Knudsen airplane.

The supplies needed by miners of all the camps came to a tremendous amount, since they traditionally ordered for a year at a time. One thing Smitty had learned during the war years was the value of larger aircraft for ferrying supplies.

Ray Shinn was vice president of Morrison-Knudsen and a very good friend, so Mudhole asked him if there was any chance of leasing the *Yellow Peril.*

The Boeing 80-A was the same one which had earned him the ribbing for being a "multiple Chinese Ace," but Smitty knew it had been changed since then. Tom Appleton, the operations engineer and chief mechanic for Morrison-Knudsen in Anchorage, had gone down to the Lockheed factory, and while he was there he found a new pair of Lodestar wheels and hydraulic brakes. The tires were not too wide to go in between the two shock struts on each wheel of the Boeing, so he brought them north and fitted them onto the *Yellow Peril.*

With these new hydraulic brakes, what had been, according to Mudhole, "just a tough line airplane," was changed into one that would stop within a thousand feet with a full load. This meant it could land on the short bush strips.

When Smitty asked Shinn if he could use the plane, his friend promptly got on the phone and checked around. He found that the *Peril* would not be needed for three weeks and said, "Sure. What are you going to do?"

"Well," said Smitty, "I got these little towns up there, and they're out of everything, and it's a tremendous amount of hauling. I could never do it with Cordova Air's one plane."

Cordova Air Service's old Stinson could haul about 450 or 500 pounds. The miners always ordered flour in 100-pound sacks, and that was only a small portion of the orders they had placed.

Mudhole Smith flew the 80-A to Cordova, rounded up all the supplies he could get there, and then flew to Chitina for more. When he figured up his load, he had about ten pounds over five tons. The legal limit for the plane was sixty-five hundred pounds, but since it was wartime, a lot of rules were routinely ignored. Smitty had flown that airplane on several occasions with a similar load, and he had no worries about it; he knew the plane could handle it.

"I went into Chisana's little fifteen-hundred-foot field with that load. It was tight, but I made it with those good brakes. The old miners came pouring out and up alongside the airplane. They'd never seen such a huge plane before.

"They kept asking, 'Did you bring my order? Did you bring my order?' and I said, 'Well, I'll tell you, anything you ordered is on here if they had it for sale.' "

Smitty invited a couple of the old fellows up in the plane, and had the rest of them pile the supplies alongside the runway. The pile looked about the size of a small house, a full year's freight in that one load.

He made several trips servicing the other small towns in that part of the country, and although they were all in need of supplies, none of them were as bad off as Chisana had been.

It was plain to Smitty that the way to handle freight was with these larger airplanes. The new runways and airports in Alaska were making it possible. The days of hauling four to five hundred pounds at a time in an open cockpit plane were just about over.

He flew to Anchorage and returned the *Yellow Peril* to Morrison-Knudsen. When he asked Ray Shinn how much he owed for the rent of the plane, he was told, "Nothing."

"But, Ray," Smitty protested, "I got money out of those trips. I'm willing to pay."

Ray said, "No, you're just getting started up again over there in Cordova and you'll need it. So you keep it."

Smitty was touched by the gesture. He had enjoyed working for Morrison-Knudsen, and now they showed that though they were a big company, they still had a heart. Smitty filled up the gas tank on the *Yellow Peril* and turned it over to the company.

In December, 1943, Merle, Bertha and Kenny spent Christmas in York, Nebraska, with Bertha's folks. She was expecting any day, and she and young son Kenny would stay with her parents while Smitty went to Fort Worth, Texas, for the first formal flying lessons he had ever taken in his life. At the American Flying School in Fort Worth, he earned his instrument flight rating. He was there for thirty days learning the techniques and took his final test on the morning of January 29, 1944.

He and the examiner landed and taxied up in front of the school's offices. As he shut off the engine, a secretary came running out to the plane.

"Mr. Smith, there's a long distance call for you, from York, Nebraska."

Smitty knew what the message would be. He jumped out of the plane and ran to the office. The call was from Bertha's mother.

"Bertha just gave birth to another fine young son for you. They're both doing fine."

So Mudhole Smith had a double reason to celebrate that day, receiving his instrument rating and becoming the father of a second son, Wayne.

He left Fort Worth the next day and went to York. Shortly afterward he took his growing family back to Cordova, where he would soon resume management of Cordova Air Service.

The Airlift

Alaska's airlines were in a state of flux following the war. Many of them that the CAB had granted routes to were now out of the picture, and others were forging ahead, trying new routes. There was such a demand for air service, Smitty recalled, that no one was quite sure what to do.

"It was just hard to tell — nobody could handle it all. So they were trying to separate the wheat from the chaff and do the best they could. That, of course, was Alaska's problem."

Some of the old stockholders of Cordova Air Service asked Smitty to come operate the airline again. He said he'd do it on one condition, that he could buy all the stockholders out. He offered them the same price that had to be repaid to the other airline when the merger was denied, thirty thousand dollars. He wanted it to be an amicable arrangement with their support. Some way or other he'd raise the money to pay them.

Most of the stockholders were getting up in age, and they wanted to sell. Some were in their seventies, others sixty to sixty-five. One of the staunchest supporters was F.A. Hansen, who had been superintendent of the railroad until it closed and he moved to Seattle. He pointed out that if they held on it meant maybe another twenty years with no dividends, and probably a lot of expense for expansion to stay in the competition.

They accepted Smitty's offer, after several months of negotiations, and for every hundred dollars they had invested in Cordova Air Service in 1934, they got back $250 in 1944. Smitty is proud that nobody associated with him in the airplane business ever lost any money.

Everybody cooperated and helped him get going again. Smitty finished up his chores with Morrison-Knudsen and replenished the supplies for the miners in the Interior. When he returned to Cordova in July of 1944, he had only one airplane in flying condition, a Bellanca that he picked up at Lake Spenard in Anchorage.

Mudhole set about acquiring planes and personnel. He bought an SM8A Stinson from Jack Peck in Anchorage, a four-place job with a 215 Lycoming engine. With these two planes he began to rebuild the bush service that had languished during the height of the war.

He hired a pilot, Daryll Underwood, called "Red," and his wife Lois as office manager. From Morrison-Knudsen he hired a mechanic, Tom Berg.

Later he added a couple of SR10 Stinsons, and from Bristol Bay Air Service he acquired an SR9 Gull-Wing Stinson, a completely modern airplane carrying four passengers and a pilot.

He began running regularly scheduled flights between Cordova and Anchorage, four times a week. Once a week he flew between Cordova and Fairbanks, making stops at Valdez, Copper Center, Gulkana, Gakona and Paxson.

Maintenance of bush airfields was often the responsibility of the airline or bush operator serving that point, and conditions remained primitive for a long time. Cordova had no terminal. Passengers rode to the airport on a drafty rattletrap bus, and huddled shivering inside the ancient machine until the airplane landed. Bob Korn, the driver, was well equipped for Alaskan conditions. He had the happy ability to slump down in his seat and fall asleep.

Mudhole hired a young pilot named Clark Cole. Clark didn't have too much experience when he came on board, but he was eager, had a lot of natural ability, and developed into a good pilot.

Clark's main assignment was to fly from Gulkana to the small strips and mines in the back country. He had a call from a miner near Slate Creek who needed to go to town for medical treatment. The miner wasn't desperately ill, but he did have an appointment with a doctor in Cordova.

Cole took off from Cordova in a small airplane equipped with an 85-hp engine. It was all he needed because he was going to haul only one passenger.

The flight to the Slate Creek area took two or three hours. Just before landing Clark radioed Cordova where he was and that he would be on the ground in a few minutes.

After that, nothing. Hours passed with no word from Cole. Haunted by visions of Cole lying on his back unable to move and the plane cracked up nearby, Mudhole prepared to fly up and see what was wrong. Just as he was to take off, a radio call came from Clark.

"I've been gone a long time, haven't I?" he asked.

"What happened? Where have you been? Are you all right?"

"Yeah, I'm all right. I'm on my way now."

"Well, what happened to you? We've been worried down here."

"Well, since I was last here to this strip, the grass has grown two feet tall. I couldn't get enough ground speed to take off in that high grass. So I had to cut a strip for a takeoff, and all I had to cut it with was a pocket knife."

He had spent eight or nine hours on the job before he had a strip long enough for takeoff. A pilot really earned his money in those days.

When he arrived in Cordova he showed the Cordova Air Service crew his hands, which were blistered and sore. Smitty said from now on he was going to send a lawn mower on Clark's flights.

Sometimes the pilots needed a snow-blower. Smitty remembers flying through the Interior in late fall with three miners. When darkness overtook them, they landed at McCarthy and spent the night. In the morning they found it had been snowing all night, and twelve to sixteen inches were piled up on the airstrip.

There was only one way to remove the snow. There were no tractors or bulldozers. Pilot and passengers alike manned big scoop shovels and worked all day. It took three solid days to clear a strip long enough for takeoff. A little later in the year, Smitty's plane would have been equipped with skis, but this was an early snow, and it caught them unexpectedly.

When they finished clearing the field, Smitty looked it over and began to grin. It reminded him of the strip Sam Gamblin had cleaned off at Horsefeld a number of years before. It was about wingspan wide where the crew began shoveling, but during three back-breaking days the shovelers gradually narrowed it until it was barely wide enough for the wheels to get through.

After Smitty got off the McCarthy field, he circled and looked down. The field came almost to a point at the end where they finished shoveling.

The snowstorm had been completely localized. McCarthy was the only place it had snowed, so if the plane had been on skis it really wouldn't have helped because all the other fields were in wheel-landing condition.

Not that the early pilots let that stop them. They often made landings and takeoffs with ski-equipped planes from mud-flats and even on slippery eel grass when they had to.

Smitty went them all one better and made headlines in the

Cordova Times with a ski landing on the gravel airstrip at Eyak
Lake. The newspaper told the story:

> Smitty had been in the Interior for ten days,
> freighting supplies with his ski-equipped plane from
> Chitina up to the miners preparing for the summer's
> work at Chisana. Finding out by radio that his pilot, Red
> Underwood, would be too busy to fly wheel equipment
> to Chitina for changing Smitty's plane over, Smitty
> decided that he would be ahead to try making a ski
> landing on Eyak's bare gravel field. He figured he might
> damage the metal covering on the bottom of the skis a
> bit, but he could replace the covering for ten bucks, and
> that was a big saving over taking the time of another
> plane in addition to the cost of gas and oil.
> So he headed down the Copper River and in due time
> swooped a greeting over the town of Cordova.
> Plane-wise Cordovans on the streets saw him coming
> in on skis. Wondering where he intended to land, with
> only the very thin ice on the lake adjacent to the air-
> field, they made a dash for their cars and headed for the
> airport, fully expecting to witness some grief on Smitty's
> part when he found only bare rocks to land on.
> But Smitty wasn't worrying much about his plight. He
> calmly wound up the stabilizer to make the ship tail
> heavy, 'gave 'er the gun' at just the right moment,
> settled on the field like a feather and came to a graceful
> stop.
> The metal bottom of the skis were scratched up a bit,
> but probably only will need to be polished up.

On one hand Smitty was caught between the need for skis,
wheels or pontoons for his various bush service points and on the
other hand he was beginning to add such stops as Anchorage,
where he needed larger, more modern aircraft.

His next acquisition was one of which he was justly proud; a 10E
Lockheed Electra, with 550-hp Pratt & Whitney engines, which he
bought from Morrison-Knudsen in Anchorage for twenty-five
thousand dollars. It was the first all-weather, twin-engine airplane
on scheduled service between Anchorage and Cordova. With it,
schedules were stepped up to six days a week, and the plane
carried eight passengers.

In February of 1946 the venerable old steamship *Yukon* struck a
rock near Seward and broke in half. The bow half clung to the
rock, with 495 persons huddled on it. Snow, sleet and the full fury
of the storm pounding the vessel hampered efforts at rescue. The
people had no water, food or shelter.

The drama heightened when Jim "Screaming Swede" Johnson,

a Cordova commercial fisherman, took a self-propelled barge alongside despite the heavy seas and began to remove those aboard. He transferred them to the Coast Guard Cutter *Onondaga* and went back for more. Then, according to news accounts, he made a line fast to his barge and rammed it ashore to pick up some survivors who had made it to land. With the tow cable, he was hauled back off the beach. This took place over a period of several days.

On the day after the shipwreck, a Cordova resident whose wife was aboard the *Yukon* came to Smitty in great agitation. He wanted to fly out and at least take a look at the ship. He knew rescue vessels were standing by, and that all that could be done was being done, but he needed to be as near as he could. He and seven others filled the Electra to capacity and they circled over the wreck taking pictures.

"Then the next day — he was frantic with worry — he chartered it again, and we went to Seward. He was going to stay in Seward and go out to the ship if there was any possible way.

"About then the survivors taken off by the Screaming Swede arrived in Seward on the *Onondaga*. When we got to Seward, she was there."

So that had a happy ending. Only 11 persons of the 371 passengers and 124 crew were lost, although everyone suffered extreme hardship and exposure. The Screaming Swede and many others contributed heroically to the rescue.

Smitty flew the Electra for a year and then sold it in Seattle. At the same time he bought a DC3, an airplane bigger than any that had been used around Cordova. He knew, along with everybody else, that there was going to be a steamship strike.

A ship strike in early Alaska was a disaster. The territory was dependent on the Alaska Steamship Company for everything. The small Alaskan towns did not, by any means, "live off the land" as popular conception had it. They were more like an army in the field, dependent upon a long and vulnerable supply line for their survival.

A ninety-day strike ten years earlier brought this home force-fully to Cordovans. People scoured the clam beaches, hunted, fished and scavenged whatever they could, wherever they could. Grocery stores were closed; there was no food to sell. Cafes served only a thin soup of reindeer meat — no butter, no eggs, very little of anything. Before the strike was over, Hunger stalked the streets.

Now, ten years later, there was to be another one. The DC3 looked mammoth to the town of Cordova when Smitty brought it in. In August, the ship strike began, and Mudhole Smith began a non-stop ferry service for groceries. He flew "outside" to Seattle one day and back the next, carrying 3½ tons of food each trip.

He put an embargo on everything but food. He supplied the entire town almost single-handedly with his airlift for the full sixty-nine days of the strike. The stores opened when Smitty's plane got in, regardless of the time. Often it was as late as midnight.

Two truckloads of food were unloaded at the stores. People lined up for a block to buy their supplies, and stayed until everything was gone and the stores closed. That happened every other night.

In Anchorage they were airlifting supplies, too, but it was all sorts of freight. Air service was more plentiful and freight could also come over the Alaska Highway. In Cordova there was only Mudhole Smith and his DC3.

In October the ships resumed running. Once again the steamers came into port with their quota of groceries, mail orders and gossip. With the strike over, Smitty's DC3 was really too big for use on the Cordova Air Service routes; there were not enough airports that could handle it. But before he had a chance to take it out and trade it for another aircraft, he had to use it again.

The Alaska Steamship Company vessel *Alaska* hit a rock on its way in to Cordova. It was not a major disaster like the *Yukon,* and damage was slight but still great enough that the company would not endanger passenger lives by carrying them any farther. The ship limped into Cordova and tied up. Next day permission came from the head office to have the passengers flown to Anchorage. There was only one DC3 in Cordova, and that was Mudhole Smith's. The charter with the steamship company came to three loads of passengers and another of baggage.

Some passengers declined to fly and stayed aboard the ship tied to the Cordova dock, awaiting the arrival of another ship to finish their voyage. It came in a few days and carried those passengers the rest of the way. The others were in Anchorage the same day the *Alaska* docked in Cordova.

Soon after this incident, Smitty flew the DC3 to Seattle and sold it. In its place he bought a Noorduyn Norseman, a ten-seat airplane, excellent for bush service.

In the late forties and early fifties, the economy of Alaska was poor and extremely seasonal. Cordova, especially, suffered from this malady. The closing of the railroad back in 1938 had finished off major mining efforts, and fishing, another seasonal industry, was now in a sharp slump. It experienced such an alarming curtailment that in 1953, 1954 and again in 1956, Prince William Sound, the mainstay of the fisheries, was closed to commercial fishing. What tourist industry there was generally came to Cordova on the Alaska Steamship Company ships, which stayed in port several hours to unload freight. Passengers trouped uptown to buy souvenirs and to take a quick look at the town.

In spite of all that, fishing remained the lifeblood of the town. Much of the service provided by Cordova Air Service was in support of the industry: flying supplies, taking fishermen to town during closed periods, and picking them up when they were sick or injured.

Emergency Medicine

Early in 1950 Mudhole Smith began to feel ill, and though he was being treated by the doctor, he seemed to get no better. When his illness was diagnosed as diabetes, his doctor grounded him.

His greatest love, flying, was denied him now. He had time to spend overseeing the operation of the airline whenever he felt up to it, which wasn't often. His condition seemed to get worse as time went by.

One Sunday he was at home alone resting when he got an urgent telephone call from a local cannery.

"Smitty, we've got an injured man out on the flats — Andy Anderson — he's in bad shape and needs to go to the hospital."

Smitty said, "Well, I'll have a pilot here in about an hour, and I'll send him right out."

He had barely lain down again before the cannery called back. "This man won't wait an hour. He got his leg caught in the bight of a line, and it's almost cut off."

Smitty said, "I'll see what I can do."

He hung up the phone and called Doctor Coffin, who was at the cannery putting up some of his own fish. The doctor had been treating Mudhole and knew to grab a few sugar cubes in case Smitty had trouble during the emergency flight.

Smitty picked him up at the cannery and the two raced to the airport. As they took off, they got part of the story from the radio, and learned the rest of it when they landed at the scene.

The tender scow *Teal* had been towing Andy Anderson's fishing skiff to town on a long tow line. On the Copper River flats the twisting channels are marked by pilings at intervals. Andy's skiff was on such a long line that it was in danger of catching on a piling, so Andy went out on deck to shorten the line. In a moment of carelessness, he stepped inside a coil of rope laying on deck.

At that moment the skiff caught a piling, the rope snapped taut and Andy's leg was nearly severed. It was hanging by only a few threads of skin. Andy whipped out his knife and cut it the rest of the way off, and the tender's crew tied on a tourniquet.

Smitty had gone from 180 pounds to 130 pounds and was very weak. When they landed at the scene, Doctor Coffin had to get out on the pontoon and help tie up the plane. Andy crawled aboard and Doctor Coffin pushed the pontoons away from the tender so Smitty could take off to the hospital.

According to Smitty, "Doc Coffin knew my condition, and that I might pass out, but he had me fly him out there anyway. Afterward, he said I was in worse shape than the passenger I brought in." It was the courage of the doctor that impressed the pilot.

Doctor Coffin ordered Smitty to show up at the hospital the next day for some tests, and within days sent him to the Mayo Clinic in Rochester, Minnesota, for an operation. While undergoing tests at Mayo, Smitty picked up a paper and read that Cap Lathrop had been killed in a mining accident at Healy. Alaska would not be the same, Smitty felt, grieving for his friend.

Just before entering the operating room, Mudhole had good news: Cordova Air Service had been named as one of thirty-six airlines in the United States awarded the coveted National Safety Council aviation safety award for 1949. Cordova Air Service had not had a single fatality on its record from the time it began scheduled flight under CAB rules and regulations.

While he was recovering from the operation, Smitty had a lot of time to think. What he thought about most was Cordova Air Service.

"We weren't getting anyplace with those single-engine airplanes. They were stopped too much of the time by weather, and had too many crack-ups and expenses. I had to go into the bigger airplanes."

When he first came to Alaska Smitty had wondered why most of the flying was in wintertime, during the worst weather and the shortest flying hours. The biggest business came when flying was the hardest.

"I wondered why we let so much good summer weather go to waste, so I tried to build up the business at that time of year."

When he got back to Cordova, Smitty worked on ideas for business expansion. With Cordova Air Service in its seventeenth year, Smity evolved a "five-year plan" that included a thirty-thousand-dollar improvement of Cordova Air Service's base at the Valdez airport, improvements at Chitina and the addition of five new ground radio stations.

In 1951 Cordova Air Service had ten airplanes in operation, of which three were dual-engine. The company employed twenty-two persons, fifteen of them in Cordova. The airline served eighteen communities including Anchorage. In the summertime it flew regular mail, passenger and supply flights to ten canneries in Prince William Sound, three times weekly.

In 1952, Smitty really got things moving. In mid-summer he completed negotiations to merge with Christiansen Flying Service, started by pioneer bush pilot Haakon Christiansen. In this merger he gained the route from Anchorage to Seward.

Smitty also received CAB permission to begin nonscheduled service from Cordova and Valdez to Fairbanks, on a trial basis to see if the traffic warranted its continuation.

This same year both Valdez and Seward airports were being upgraded to handle DC3 aircraft. It all fitted together nicely with the expansion ideas Smitty had in mind. Still, to keep a DC3 busy would take some innovative ideas. It was a big airplane, considering the state of the territory's feeble economy.

In the fall of 1952 Smitty and Bertha went to California and visited her uncle while a plane was being overhauled. One Sunday they went out to see Knott's Berry Farm. During the tour around the place, a thought occurred to Mudhole. He said to himself, "Well, doggone, this looks kind of like McCarthy. If they're pulling in tourists here, why can't I do the same thing with tourists at McCarthy? It's there already, I don't have to do anything to it.

"As it happened, before I even left California I got a letter from McCarthy, from people named Brown. They wanted to get one of the buildings and open up what they called the McCarthy Lodge. It was the old Hubrick house that I had bought, and these people wanted to fix it up. I thought, there's the answer to a prayer. I'd been wondering how I was going to get more use out of the DC3 — when I got one — and this was it. I could run into McCarthy on Saturday morning and come out on Sunday evening, and the Browns could keep the people overnight.

"So they opened the lodge. Later I went ahead and bought the old Golden, J.B. O'Neill's store, and fixed it up as a hotel and saloon.

"The McCarthy weekends were a success right from the start. We hauled nine hundred passengers the first year, only we started going in Friday night at seven o'clock, leaving Anchorage and landing at May Creek."

May Creek was twenty-five miles from McCarthy. The field there could handle a DC3, but the dirt road into McCarthy was badly in need of repair. Most of the bridges were down, and Cordova Air Service had to repair them.

"We fixed up an old Model T truck with wooden benches in the back and we hauled them to town in that. We also fixed up another one at Kennicott. We mounted it on railroad wheels and called it the 'Kennecott Express.' Governor Gruening got the Interior Department to set that railroad aside as a tourist attraction.

"We had demands for DC3 loads from Valdez to McCarthy, and one weekend we had a DC3 load from Fairbanks and from Anchorage another time. We had more than seventy people in there on one weekend. The town really came alive then, and land values soared. Everybody got interested in McCarthy."

It was something Smitty came to feel very strongly about, the building of Alaska communities and their economy through air transportation.

In December of 1952, two airports, both important to Smitty, were improved. They were at Valdez and Seward, two points on Smitty's route. They had been enlarged enough to accommodate a DC3, and Governor Gruening dedicated them. Smitty bought a DC3 for Cordova Air Service at that time, and flew people to the ceremonies free of charge.

The DC3 changed the pace of development for Cordova Air Service and the communities it served.

"The first DC3 I bought, back in 1946, I never intended to use on scheduled flights. This second one I bought with the idea of using it on nothing but schedules, because Governor Gruening and Tony Schwamm, head of the Department of Aviation, had started a program to enlarge other airports in the smaller Alaska towns. Seward and Valdez got their fields fairly early. A couple of years later the field at Chitina could take a DC3, and they had one big enough at May Creek. The Yakataga field had been there since the war, and it was a busy stop."

The DC3 was an aircraft almost three times as big as the ones Smitty used previously. Buying it represented a large gamble. It can be argued, and Smitty would be the last to deny it, that his devotion to the development of the economy in Southcentral Alaska's small communities helped build up his own airline. But because the two were so inextricably interwoven, the prosperity and survival of Cordova Air Service was equivalent to the prosperity and survival of the communities it served. There simply was no way to separate the two.

However, Smitty gave attention to more than the economics and building of the business. There were the sports, too — the free or near-free basketball trips, the moose and fish transplants, the Shrine Circus trips and the dog sled racing. Mudhole Smith was a great supporter of sports of all kinds.

Getting in the Ol' Ball Game

A whole generation of Alaskans grew up with a lore of intercity basketball games sponsored by Mudhole Smith and Cordova Air Service — sometimes free, sometimes at greatly reduced rates. There were flights to Valdez, Seward, Glennallen, Anchorage, Fairbanks.

The kids (now grown up) tell stories of basketball trips that Smitty made possible in one way or another. The rivalry between Valdez and Cordova was especially intense.

"Remember the old Valdez gym? The stage was at one end of the floor, and the steps leading into the gym were at the other, so close there was no out-of-bounds. The kids watching the game sat up on the stage or along the sides of the floor. When you came driving down the floor for a lay-up, you either cracked your ribs on the edge of the stage or fell down the stairs."

"Yeah. One time Bill Reid, a Cordova player, came driving down the floor for a lay-up, hit the stage and slid right up on top across it. Bill was all tangled up in flying kids and chairs."

"I wouldn't have minded that," Bill said, "but the kids started kicking me while I was lying there. They were Valdez rooters." Feelings ran high at the games.

"And then Bud drove down to the other end, fell down the stairs and broke a tooth. . . ."

"And, hey, remember those warped backboards? The Cordova team was taught to bounce their shots off the backboard into the basket, but if you did that in Valdez, they never went in. Cordova wasn't scoring. The rules then were that you couldn't call time out and huddle. It wasn't until half-time that the coach could tell the team to quit using the back-boards.

"How about the time Smitty's plane brought over half of the team, but the pilot was new and not used to the approach to the Valdez field. He hit a little updraft coming in for his first landing, so he pulled his wheels up and poured on the coal, figuring on going around again. Just then he broke out of the updraft and found himself in perfect position for landing after all, so he brought it on in. But he forgot that his wheels were up and he made a belly landing. So half the team was stranded in Valdez and the other half was left in Cordova.

The small coastal communities of Alaska have always been strong on basketball. The climate is too wet and cold for football to thrive as a popular sport, and the summertime is too busy with fishing and cannery work for baseball. But basketball is played indoors, at a season when people have time to go watch the games and root for the home team. Kids just big enough to run begin to practice their basketball shots and dribbling. The intercity games promoted by Mudhole Smith became the major sport.

"You know why we did that, don't you?" asked Smitty. "In the early days the only basketball we had in the region was the school playing the town team, the Elks and other clubs that put together a team. The schools never got to play anybody of their own age and caliber. Maybe once a year they would get a trip to some other town, usually on a fishing boat. The whole team, like as not, would get seasick on the trip over.

"We were the first to start flying the kids back and forth between Cordova and Valdez. Then we worked up some rivalry between Seward and Cordova. They played a series of games. Finally I got Anchorage to come over by giving them a free trip. The town turned out at the gymnasium, and the Anchorage kids were thrilled to death because they had such an enormous crowd and were so royally entertained. That led to its being a two-way street, Cordova to Anchorage and Anchorage to Cordova, and that went on for years.

"When the Glennallen school started, we included them, and the Copper Valley School. We had kids from all over the country. We were the ones who started such exchanges.

"A principal in Anchorage told me that during one of their meetings regarding sports schedules, the Fairbanks school objected because it was going to cost them too much money for transportation. The principal explained, 'We don't have a Cordova Airlines.'"

Mudhole Smith still considers that a tribute of some sort, and is greatly pleased to recall it.

"Every weekend I was flying free trips, getting basketball teams either in or out of Cordova, and I also took at least one load of underprivileged kids to the Shrine Circus in Anchorage every year. They gave me a lifetime membership pass for all functions in the Cordova schools. I've still got that, although I never used it."

Smitty started flying teams to different cities very early. An article in the Ketchikan paper told of a 1940 basketball trip to a tournament in Fairbanks. The Cordova basketball team was called the "Cordova Clamdiggers." Smitty recalled "Nobody expected anything of the Clamdiggers, but they came in second. They missed first by two points."

A free trip for the children to the Shrine Circus in Anchorage was a yearly event provided by Mudhole Smith. In 1956 the children flew in a DC3. (Photograph by Ward Wells, courtesy of Merle Smith)

Basketball was not the only sport supported by Mudhole Smith. The Cordova Airlines women's bowling team named themselves "The Mudholers."

Dog racing was another activity supported by Smitty. He sponsored a dog team for the Fur Rendezvous races several years in a row.

Sometimes Smitty paid for his sports-minded generosity in other ways than loss of fares. Ken Van Brocklin, who laughingly says that he "has caught more hell from Mudhole than anyone in Alaska," told of a time the Elks basketball team wanted to go to Valdez.

"We asked Smitty if we could use his plane for seven ballplayers, with Red Underwood as pilot. Then the day before we left I said, 'God, Smitty, we're really stuck. We've only got Vince Addington, who's the referee, and barely enough ballplayers. Could Red leave the plane there and play the game with us?'

Mudhole strongly supported athletic events and helped develop intercity high school competition by providing free transportation for school sports teams. This service was also provided Cordova's dog sled team. (Photograph by Forrest and Helen Shields, courtesy of Merle Smith)

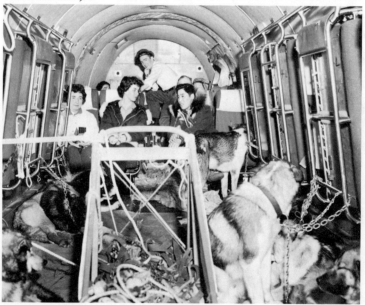

"He said, 'Well, it's against my better judgment. I need that plane real bad, but go ahead.' He gave us all a round-trip ticket for just $7.50 apiece.

"So we flew to Valdez and Red played with us. But the weather closed in that night.

"*Nine days later* — I'm not kidding — nine days later, the weather broke so we could get back. We survived in Valdez thanks to the generosity of Truck Egan and Bill Egan, who financed us when we all went broke. And Smitty was over there in Cordova needing a plane and a pilot who could have been making money for him all those nine days.

"When the weather cleared, Red came to me and said, 'Kenny, you're on the first flight. I don't want to face Smitty alone.' I says, 'No, I'm not. I don't want to face him either. I'm going down to the Pinzon Bar to wait while you take the first load over, and I'll be able to tell when you get there because I'll hear Smitty clear from there.'

"We were down at the Pinzon Bar and after about an hour-and-a-half there was a big roar outside. Someone asked, 'What was that?' It was probably a car, but I said, 'Well, Red Underwood just landed in Cordova and Smitty met the plane.'

"When I saw Smitty again, he said, 'Van Brocklin, you'll never again get anything from me. No plane, no nothing.' So about two weeks later we needed a plane to go to Fairbanks with the team, and he says with a growl, 'Yeah, you so-and-so, go ahead.' "

Several decades earlier, Doc Chase had planted Sitka blacktail deer on Hawkins Island near Cordova, where they thrived and spread to neighboring islands, furnishing fall hunting for sportsmen and venison for the tables of Cordova.

Inspired by the success of the deer transplants, the Isaac Walton League began a project to plant moose on the Copper River flats.

The Cordova area had no moose because two glaciers up at Mile 49 cut off access down the Copper River to the flats. The moose had no way to get into the lower Copper River delta where there was plenty to browse.

Hollis Henrich, the local postmaster, was the spark plug for the whole deal, and also acted as nursemaid for the arriving baby moose, which Smitty agreed to fly over from Kenai at no charge.

"We took them out of Kenai into Anchorage, put them onto one of our scheduled DC3 flights and unloaded them in Cordova onto a truck. They were hauled to a pen and kept for a few weeks, then were turned loose on the Copper River flats.

Mudhole also cooperated with the Isaac Walton League in an effort to transplant moose into the Copper River flats. To help he flew baby moose into the flats. Chicken wire corrals had to be installed between the pilots and the moose to keep the animals from making meals of the fliers' jackets.

"We built a little pen out of ropes in the front end of the DC3 cabin and loaded the passengers right in with the baby moose.

"One day a member of the CAB was in Anchorage, and I thought he would enjoy seeing these little moose in the airplane. But in getting them corraled up front, we delayed the flight ten minutes. I had expected him to hand me some bouquets, but he chewed me out for about forty-five minutes over our unrealistic schedules. From then on I was very careful not to delay a flight when one of those big shots was in the country, even if being ten or fifteen minutes late was more sensible than starting by the clock.

"On one trip, the moose calves got out of their corral and wandered up in the cockpit with the pilots. They nosed around and chewed on the tails of the pilots' coats, hanging over the seat backs, and on their shirts. A baby moose can strip the back off a shirt in a couple of good nibbles, so the pilots were slapping at them and trying to shoo them away. The stewardess played it real smart and stayed in the rear of the airplane and let the pilots be stewardesses for the moose.

"After that escapade, I had to put some chicken wire between the cockpit and the moose pens, to keep them from trying to get up there and help fly the plane.

"Doc Chase was also the go-between with the Fish & Wildlife Service in setting up fish transplants to stock the lakes around Cordova, some of which had not had fish in them for years. The techniques were not so far advanced then as they are now. All they'd do is get some fingerlings, we'd fly them in tanks, and they'd just take them out and dump them in a lake. It worked, though. In a year or two we started catching some good-sized fish. Some of the lakes have fish today because of the transplants done by that group of men and Cordova Airlines.

"There was no money for the project. Everything was a donation, including the flying."

When Doc Chase got the idea to stock the lakes around Cordova with fingerling fish, Mudhole was there to help and fly the fish over the lakes where they were dumped. Their efforts, though not sophisticated, had excellent results and large fish were caught the next year. Here Mudhole prepares to load the fish.

Rabbits on Middleton Island came later, after Cordova Air Service added that tiny, low-lying island far out in the Gulf of Alaska to its routes.

"One of my crews took several pair of rabbits — there were no rabbits on Middleton Island — that he bought with his own money and transplanted on Middleton. It has a rank growth of grass, and even after it died and fell down, the rabbits had food all winter long.

"I don't know how many hunters of rabbits there are on Middleton Island today, but we used to fly hunting parties out there. Rabbits are plentiful because there are no predators, no mink, otter, coyote or wolves.

"The same pilot tried to plant some chukkers there. They remind me of Cornish game hens only they don't have big feathers. They're real good eating. On our first rabbit hunting trip, one of the hunters was seen stuffing some chukkers into his hunting sack along with the rabbits he'd shot, before the birds had a chance to get started on the island.

"About this time the Fish & Game notified us that we were doing something illegal by planting 'exotic' species out there, so we quit. But I often wonder why the Fish & Game didn't go ahead with that idea. They could have closed the rabbit season for a while and planted chukkers or quail, and I think they'd have done real well."

The Copper Nugget

In 1953 Cordova Air Service again won the Aviation Safety Award, as it had the previous year. Smitty was in the process of a vigorous expansion program. In keeping with the new dimension of service offered by the airline, he changed the name from Cordova Air Service to Cordova Airlines.

"If I had realized how many things had to be changed when you change an airline's name, I might not have done it," he growled. "The tickets, the baggage tags, stationery, everything. It takes a lot more trouble than had ever occurred to me."

1953 and 1954 saw the biggest expansion ever in Cordova Airlines. By the merger with Christiansen Air, Smitty had acquired a short but important route from Anchorage to Seward (seventy-five miles). He added the daily flights to Fairbanks, and the airline had about a thousand miles of routes.

Anchorage's new International Airport was in use by October of

1953, and Cordova Airlines moved that end of its operations over from Merrill Field. When Smitty's new hangar was put into use, there was only one other commercial hangar at the field — Northern Consolidated Airways.

In 1954 Phillips Petroleum started drilling in the Icy Bay area, and needed DC3 service to Yakataga almost full-time, so Smitty added a second plane to his growing fleet.

"That's the way I've found it all my life," said Smitty. "Alaska communities are down today and up tomorrow. Gillam used to point this out to me. I heard him say many a time that, geographically speaking, Alaska is not yet settled. He was right then, and it's the truth to this day. What is a village today may become a booming town tomorrow, and what's a big town today is a nothing tomorrow — we've had that happen.

"Seward stays about the same in population. Kenai has grown a lot, but is less important on air routes, mostly because of the road. Soldotna didn't exist until comparatively few years ago, and now it's a good-sized community. McCarthy was a booming community, now you have thirty or forty people there. Same way with Chitina. And Chisana, which used to be quite a lively little mining camp. When I first went to Chisana there were about a hundred people living there the year round, now I doubt if there's ten.

"So the country just isn't settled yet, in any long-range predictable pattern, and I don't know when it ever will be."

The DC3, in addition to its other talents, could handle some rather exotic cargo. For instance, there was a fifty-five-hundred-pound copper nugget so dense it was smaller than a bathtub.

"Some promoters had a lay for mining — what they call a lay was a lease on a share basis — on Dan Creek Mine. When they found this great big copper nugget, they thought that by getting it out whole and bringing it to Anchorage to put in front of their office, they could sell a lot of stock in their mine. Alaska was still a territory and everything was blue sky in that respect.

"They wanted to hire Cordova Airlines to fly it to Anchorage. I went up and took a look at it, and I wasn't too crazy about the job, but I finally agreed to do it. It weighed nearly three tons all in one hunk, and was most difficult to handle.

"We had to be sure it was right on the plane's center of gravity. We went inside the plane and measured it to find the exact spot.

"At the mine they used block-and-tackle and a tractor to put it on a flatbed truck. They backed the truck up even with the door of the plane — it happened to be the same height — and just slid it off.

Sounds easy, but it wasn't because it was so heavy and compact. Only so many people could gather around to pry on it. We had to work it forward into the exact center of gravity. Because the DC3 tail wheel was slanted downhill when it was on the ground, we had to work the nugget forward uphill, and it was one awful task because we had no come-alongs, no hoists or anything out there in the tules. It was just by brute strength that we pried it up there an eighth of an inch at a time.

"To get it tied down secure was no easy chore either. We took some of the floor-boards out and actually lashed it to the frame of the airplane because the regular cargo fasteners didn't look strong enough to hold it if we got into some turbulent air.

"Flying it back was touchy. Normally, if you're trimmed out right and your nose comes down a little, it'll just gradually come back up. With that heavy weight, the nose would just keep going down. Compensate for that and pretty soon the tail would be going down and you'd have to adjust for that. So it was work all the way, with the plane slowly rocking along through the sky.

"In Anchorage they had trucks and equipment to put it in front of their office. However, the promotion of the Dan Creek Mine didn't work out for the lease holders. The owners, Jack O'Niell and his nephews, took possession of the nugget and displayed it for a long time at the Anchorage Chamber of Commerce's log cabin. Eventually it was given to the University of Alaska and is now in the museum, right in the hallway as you go in. It's the first thing you see as you step in the door."

For the Horses of Chisana

Chisana was a good hunting area for big game. There were guides there with pack trains, and they had to get horse feed brought in.

"Horses need alfalfa meal. It's good for their kidneys or something," Smitty said. "That stuff came in great big sacks, which weighed a hundred pounds, but so bulky you could get only two or three sacks in a bush airplane. And then for rough feed they had to have baled hay, which is also bulky. I thought that if I could extend the strip, a DC3 could handle that kind of freight just fine."

The territory had extended the field at Chitina by this time, and Smitty tried to get them to do the same at Chisana, which had a bush strip fifteen hundred feet long, too short for a DC3.

"The FAA engineers and the Territory of Alaska made a survey there and estimated the cost of building it at $150,000. It was out of the question. They didn't have that kind of money. So we built it, and the total cost was $3,500.

"However, it turned out that it took a long time to extend that field. First, one of the old-timers died, and I bought his Caterpillar tractor. It didn't have a bulldozer blade on it. It was just a little old gasoline tractor. I ordered a blade from the Northern Commercial Company. They had to make it special, and it cost a fortune. Then I found out the bulldozer blade required a yoke too big to tie on the outside of the bush airplane. A couple of years later Einar Johnson got a Cat in, and I hired him to knock out a semblance of a field. We were finally able to make a DC3 landing with the big yoke. We fixed up our tractor and a pretty good runway.

"Then one of the creeks — Bonanza Creek, I think it was — flooded over. We took the Cat and cut the water off with a big dike. It's still there and the field has not flooded since. The fifty-seven-hundred-foot strip is still used.

"We didn't finish it until 1957, late in the year when there were several loads of horse feed to be taken in. We told the guides they would have to order their horse feed early enough next year so that we could get it in by October. We weren't going to remove the snow to keep the field open.

"Now that they could get horse feed, the guides got more horses. The second year after the field was completed, the pack trains grossed sixty-five thousand dollars from hunters.

"That was building the economy, and the DC3s did it. It was my whole point and effort there, to get modern transportation into the outlying areas. We had to develop the little communities because they were all we had. The Civil Aeronautics Act of 1938 specifically charged us with doing that very thing."

There was no question of the place aviation held in Alaska when on September 24, 1954, the Alaska Steamship Company's *Denali* sailed from Pier 42 in Seattle to Alaska on the last passenger trip. The voyage ended regular passenger trade that had begun in 1895 and was deeply ingrained as a part of Alaska's history. From then on, Alaska steamships carried only freight.

The steamships had done an outstanding job, but by their nature they were limited. The airlines had to finish the job once the goods and passengers reached the shores of Alaska. It was simply inevitable as airlines evolved, gaining in speed, range and safety, and as airports improved to accommodate the bigger aircraft.

THE
LATER
YEARS

Dawson Excursions

Vandalism was rampant in the old ghost towns of Alaska in the late fifties and early sixties, and the destruction was destroying their tourist value. Little could be done about it because many of the towns that could be attractions didn't really belong to anyone, and others belonged to people who didn't like tourists.

The McCarthy-Kennecott tours went well for about five years. The "Kennecott Express," the Model T truck with flanges on the wheels so it could travel over the old Copper River & North-western Railway tracks to the Kennecott mines, moved at four or five miles an hour and the riders really had a chance to enjoy the scenery along the way. The truck pulled another car behind it and the whole thing was very popular.

"Then the Kennecott people sold the surface rights to the mine. The people who bought the land didn't like tourists and closed the mine to visitors. We could still travel on the old railroad because the right-of-way had been set aside as a tourist attraction by the Department of the Interior but we couldn't allow the visitors to get off the cars. All but the roadbed was private property.

A trip to Knott's Berry Farm gave Mudhole the idea that such a tourist attraction could be developed at the Kennecott Mine. Here the Kennecott Express brings a load of youngsters out to the mine. (Courtesy of O.A. Nelson)

"Even that restriction wasn't enough for the new owners. About 1964 or 1965 during the winter they bulldozed the rails off the bed in spite of what the Interior Department had said about the railroad being a tourist monument. They wanted to put a road over the route and eventually did.

"I had to look other places for a summer tourist attraction in our service area. I drove to Dawson City, on the Yukon in Canada. It was just what I was looking for, but we weren't very well received when my sales manager and I went there early in June to talk to the businessmen about our bringing in tourists. Others from Alaska had tried it, and it seems the bills had not been paid. The Dawson people were left with a bad taste in their mouth.

"We finally convinced them we meant business. We started flying tourists in on the longest day of the year, June 21st.

"We were fortunate in getting the wife of the manager of the Northern Commercial Company to be our agent there. We put a thousand dollars in the bank. She was the only one who could write checks on it, and she would go around every month and pay all the bills. The tours were a package that included a hotel room, and we paid the hotels. It didn't take long before we had a good reputation.

"We booked eighty persons for the first excursion. The Governor of Alaska, Bill Egan, and his wife consented to go along to promote good will. The mayor of Anchorage, George Beyers, and several outstanding citizens of that city and from western Alaska also went as the airline's guests to help promote the tours, and it was a huge success.

"The women of Dawson City had been trying to draw tourists to Dawson for a number of years, so they especially greeted us. They dressed up in their old style clothes, met us at the airport, which was six miles out of town, and made everybody feel more than welcome.

"Business thereafter was excellent. We flew to Dawson every weekend, never with less than fifty passengers. They, too, got into the spirit of the thing and dressed up for the trip. Northern Commercial Co. employees in Anchorage dressed up in Gay Nineties costumes when they chartered a plane. Fifty of them went on that special trip and were met by the ladies of Dawson who had a band at the airport. That was a real big weekend.

"We had excellent cooperation from the Canadian government and the citizens of Dawson. We divided the business as best we could among the hotels so everybody would get a piece of the action. It was not very long before we were having difficulty finding rooms; our business got so good we were filling everything up. And I don't remember ever having one complaint from any passenger, about not having a good time in Dawson City.

"We had a T-Category 46 that could carry fifty passengers and two DC3s that would carry twenty-eight and thirty respectively. Next we found ourselves using bush equipment to make trips with three to five persons during the week, almost every day.

"We had excellent cooperation from the customs in Dawson and also the United States customs in Anchorage. Northway was another customs station where we could clear passengers if they got off short of Anchorage, say, at Gulkana. With such friendly attitudes on both sides, it was a real pleasure to fly into Dawson City.

"Then the Canadian federal government came through and rebuilt the old Palace Grand Theatre, a three-story building put up by Arizona Charlie Meadows in the 1890s. Meadows went from Arizona to Dawson City in its heyday and built a big dance hall he called the Palace Grand. It was pretty well run down when the Canadian government restored it, and they spent half a million dollars on the project. They did a good job. They drove steel pilings through the permafrost to solid rock, so it's got a perfect foundation, and it never will tumble down.

"The theater was finished about two years after we began flying in there. It opened with the premier of a play called *Foxy*, starring Bert Lahr and Beatrice Lilly along with other show names from Hollywood, New York and even Paris. The play had a northern setting and it went over real well. Afterward it ran on Broadway for five years.

"During that time a lot of people from Washington, D.C., took the trouble to go to New York to see *Foxy*, because they had heard so much about it through our advertising of the tours. So *Foxy* was a real success and so was Dawson City as far as Cordova Airlines was concerned, and I'm sure the tourist business was a real success for the people of Dawson because they all made money.

"I think it was the Bank of Montreal where we put that thousand dollars to pay Dawson City bills. They had just sent a young man

When uncooperative landowners put an end to Mudhole's Kennecott Express, he was forced to find another attraction. What he found proved grander than he ever expected, benefiting himself and the town of Dawson City, YT. Here he takes a group of people dressed in Gay Nineties attire for a weekend in historic Dawson. (Photograph by Ward Wells, courtesy of Merle Smith)

up from Toronto or some eastern Canadian city to run the bank. He was a nice young man, very civic-minded. He met the planes and did everything he could to help us on the weekends, so we opened our checking account in his bank. One night he invited us over for a cup of coffee or a drink, me, our sales manager and our wives, and he showed us a letter he had received from his main office.

"They congratulated him on the wonderful strides he had made in his new job as manager of the Dawson City branch, especially in securing such a large deposit from an American company. I had to laugh to myself, it was only a thousand dollars, but we did put a lot of cash through the account from ticket sales in Dawson. We had authority from both the Canadian government and the U.S. Civil Aeronautics Board to fly passengers between Dawson City and Anchorage.

"That almost back-fired. The people of Dawson soon got wise that they could take our airline to Anchorage and fly south, and Canadian Pacific was getting hurt by it. They were making only three DC3 flights a week from Whitehorse to Dawson.

"I thought I'd better head off complaints from Canadian Pacific Air. I knew Grant McConaghey, an old bush pilot from that area who was president of the airline. I went to Vancouver to talk with him. It turned out he was tickled to death with our going in there and promoting, they had done more business than ever before, all they could handle. The little business that we took away wasn't hurting them a bit.

"So all in all it was one of the best relationships we had with any town, city or country."

Mudhole Smith's two boys were growing up. "Kenny and Wayne were interested in being pilots from practically the day they were born," Smitty said. "I enjoyed taking them around in some of the smaller planes like the Aeronca Sedan.

"Wayne, being the littlest, had to sit in the back seat. Kenny got to hold the controls on level flight. When it came time to land, I'd tell him to take his hands off the wheel and his feet off the rudder and I'd take over.

"Well, that worked all right with Kenny, but when Wayne got old enough to be allowed to do that, he wouldn't take his hands off. He'd fight 'er all the way through, right until she was on the ground. He reminded me of myself when I was trying to learn to fly back in Kansas. Any minute I wasn't holding the controls it was a lost cause. It looked as though he felt the same way."

By the sixties, Mudhole's sons were pretty well grown. Kenny went away to college. With a year to go at the University of Alaska, he decided he'd like to get a commercial pilot's license.

"I thought a lot about this," said Mudhole. "I just sort of grew up with aviation. I didn't know anything about navigation nor even how to read a compass when I soloed. I learned that myself, and more about it after I came to Alaska. It had taken me seven or eight years, by trial, error and listening to older pilots, to learn which way you kicked your rudder to make it turn left or right.

"There was no need for the boys to go through similar experiences. I told Kenny, 'Well, if you're going to learn to fly, you better go down to Fort Worth, where I got my instrument rating. Take a full commercial test down there, and your instrument rating, so you'll be a really accomplished pilot.' So he did, and he got good grades.

"When Wayne came along, he did the same thing, with the same results. They both were good students and I got letters from Reed Pigman, who had given me my instrument rating, telling me what fine boys they were and what excellent pilots they would be. Naturally I was happy."

Both of them flew for Cordova Airlines for a while. Still, having a father in the same business must have been a trial at times. On one occasion I heard Mudhole growl that when Wayne parked a plane, he tied it down "with just a shoestring!"

Earthquake!

On March 27, 1964, one of the most severe earthquakes ever recorded shook southcentral Alaska for five-and-a-half minutes. When it was over a huge tidal wave rampaged along the coast, spreading death, destruction and terror. The epicenter of the quake was in Prince William Sound, where the land, above or below water, was shoved upward in places as much as thirty-three feet, while in other places it sunk six or seven feet.

"Cordova came out relatively unharmed," Smitty recounted. "Cordova Airlines escaped without any damage at Eyak Lake so our bush pilots, Jim Osborne in particular, were out the next morning. Osborne flew the Super Widgeon, accompanied by an observer, and they went all around the sound to see how people in the cabins had made out.

"Some cabins were completely gone — the tidal wave had taken

ere was no sign of life. One that had disappeared was
, a trapper well known in Cordova.

over Chenega, the only building they saw left was the
se. Earlier, a military plane had flown over Chenega on
the same mission, to survey damage and find out if anyone needed
help in the isolated places. The pilot, not being familiar with
Chenega and what it had looked like before the earthquake, didn't
know the whole village had been wiped out. He saw the
schoolhouse and people around it, so he reported that Chenega
had survived and everything was fine.

"Osborne landed immediately, and all the people who had
survived came down to the beach.

"Their food had been destroyed. They did have a roof over their
heads, the schoolhouse. It is still there, on a high hill above the
village, but in their fear most of them had spent the night farther
up the mountain, where they huddled around a campfire.

"The Super Widgeon is a six-place airplane but a good load
carrier. To make room for survivors, Jim left the observer and
took off with seventeen men, women and kids packed into the
plane. He flew them into Cordova, then went back with food and
other supplies so those still there could live in the schoolhouse. On
that return he brought back more of the younger children and
their mothers. He made another trip or two that day and by the
day following the earthquake, had taken everybody out.

"I've always marveled how he was able to lift that Widgeon off
the water with seventeen people in it," Smitty said. "Of course
nobody had any baggage — they had nothing left to bring — and
none of them weighed very much. With the kids and all, three of
them equaled the weight normally assigned on the plane for one
passenger with luggage so it wasn't as much as it sounds. Still,
anybody will agree that seventeen persons must be a record
number for a Super Widgeon.

"In Anchorage we had quite a bit of damage to our main
hangar. Thousands of dollars worth of instruments were shaken
off the shelves. Our airplanes, though, were undamaged.

"All communications were out, along with the power. The only
way we could find out what had happened to places on our routes,
such as Soldotna and Seward, was just to go there.

"We tried to make every town the next day. We discouraged
people from going along until we knew more about the situation,
but some had families in the towns and insisted they had to go. We
took them, but we brought more people back the other way.

"We had the old T-Category 46 that could carry fifty passengers, and we took load after load of passengers out of Soldotna. They all wanted to get out of Alaska, and most of them headed for Seattle as fast as the stateside planes could haul them. Those airlines put on extra flights and handled them about as fast as we brought them to Anchorage.

"The terminal building had been destroyed so we had to turn the cargo rooms in our hangar into passenger waiting rooms. We had only one toilet out there and it was working overtime. We piled our cargo on the hangar floor, and left some of the bigger cargo outside. For a few days we just couldn't handle all the stuff that we had to haul there.

"The only good thing about it was that our gross in cash went up about three thousand dollars a day. It really helped financially, because everybody was demanding cash from everybody else. It was a tough way, though, to have to earn it.

"They gradually got the roads fixed so people could get back into Valdez, Seward, Kenai and Soldotna. We were happy to have the load taken off."

Alaska gradually settled back to normal and rebuilt. In August of 1964, Smitty finally secured the route he had been seeking for many years, the route to Juneau. Actually, it was an extension of the Yakutat run.

Trying to get certification for this route was particularly frustrating for Mudhole. He remembered that back in 1939 he could have had it simply by saying yes to the right question. Cordova Air Service held grandfather rights then, having flown the Southeastern route many times, but when asked if he wanted it, Smitty could only think of its difficulties and overlooked its promise. By saying no twenty-five years earlier, he now had to spend thousands of dollars to obtain what he could have had for nothing.

The process had begun in 1958 with a strategy meeting between Mudhole and his advisers. They commissioned the necessary studies, and these confirmed their opinion that Juneau could use service from another carrier.

Cordova Airlines began gathering data, going through the lengthy preparations to apply to the CAB for a hearing. Juneau civic leaders assured the airline of support from the community during the hearings, and after three years they got under way in Anchorage.

Witnesses favorable to Cordova Airlines' cause appeared from all the towns along the route: Cordova, Yakutat and the coastal villages in between. Things looked good as the hearings moved to Juneau.

There it didn't go so well. Another airline had protested the route award, and the promised support from the community of Juneau failed to materialize. Not one witness from Juneau spoke in favor, although there was support from neighboring towns. The result was a denial of the application. Cordova Airlines had lost Round One.

Cordova Airlines' lawyer in Washington, D.C., kept working on the case and in due time the CAB reversed the decision of the judge and awarded the Yakutat-Juneau route to Cordova.

Late Friday afternoon, Washington, D.C., time (which made it midday in Alaska), Smitty got a phone call from Bill Bart, the attorney: "Congratulations, Smitty." The entire process had taken nearly six years. Cordova Airlines began flying the Juneau run in August with two new Convairs.

The increase in subsidy was only sixty-four thousand dollars, not in line with other subsidies being paid but "we were able to survive with it," said Smitty.

"It seems we stepped on everybody's toes with that route," says Mudhole. "We served champagne and somebody in our sales department got the idea of advertising it as the Champagne Flight, but Western Airlines had that name copyrighted, and immediately took exception."

They ceased using the name for the flights, but not the champagne. It was still being served on the flights when Cordova merged with Alaska Airlines in 1968.

The jets had come to Alaska. When Pacific Northern Airlines brought its first Boeing 720A jet to Anchorage, five of the legendary bush pilots posed under the wing of an old Travel Air, with the big shiny jet in the background. They were Art Woodley, Bob Reeve, Ray Petersen, Jim Dodson and Mudhole Smith. With them was manager of Anchorage International Airport, Tony Schwamm, who had been in the forefront of efforts to extend the smaller Alaskan airstrips to accommodate DC3s.

Now these same airfields were further extended to take the big jets. Alaska Airlines, on the merger with Cordova Airlines took the Convairs off the Juneau run and put on Boeing 727s.

Mudhole Smith, the kid from Kansas who had built his own first plane and taught himself to fly, had gone from the barnstorming era into the jet age, and now he was ready to retire.

Grandparents

Both of Smitty's sons had been flying for Cordova Airlines until the time of the merger, so they were faced with the question of what to do afterward.

Kenny wanted to live in Anchorage, so he decided to go to work in Alaska Airlines' sales department. He didn't want to fly the mainline jets and Alaska Air did very little bush flying. Eventually he became manager of Anchorage International Airport, but later he transferred to the state's Department of Aviation.

"Alaska Air wanted to dispose of the bush operations," Smitty said, "so the new owners sold that part of Cordova Airlines, along with several airplanes and the old hangar, back to Wayne. They gave him a contract to fly the bush mail runs they still retained and since then he's flown pretty regular."

By now Smitty and Bertha were grandparents. Kenny and Donna Sandstrom of Cordova were married in 1963 and the first grandchild was Pamela, followed by Weston.

In 1967 Wayne married Diann Davis, another Cordova girl, and they, too, added two grandchildren to the collection: Patsy and Skyler.

Skyler was about three years old when he made his first effort to fly, with spectacular results. Smitty said, "Since his father, his grandfather and his uncle Wayne all fly, he is naturally very interested in airplanes.

"One rainy Sunday afternoon they were at the Eyak Airport. It was storming real bad, so all the planes were in the hangar. We kind of stacked them in, so Wayne's 180's wing was over the motor on Kenny's Cub.

"Weston's mother was running the radio and doing office work. Weston loved to go out and sit in Daddy's Cub, so she would put him in it and he would sit there all afternoon, making airplane noises like he was flying.

"Unfortunately, that Sunday, his Uncle Wayne had flown the airplane the day before. He had cut the ignition switch but not the master switch which disconnected the battery from the entire electrical system. Weston had watched his father and his uncle often enough and he knew they pushed this little button on the dash to make it start. He was very much living the life of a pilot, getting ready to start his engine to take off. So he pushed the little button and the prop flew around and hit the wing above and knocked a fair-sized hole in Uncle Wayne's 180.

"Of course they heard it all over the hangar and came a-running. Poor little Weston, he was still sitting up in the front seat, hanging onto the stick, his eyes big as saucers. He didn't say a word to anybody. His mother reached in and pulled him out, but all he got was a little loving for being safe. Wayne learned better than to leave the switch on around little boys."

Smitty had not flown commercially for many years, and very little otherwise due to physical limitations. One day Weston and Pamela were talking airplanes. Neither child had ever seen their grandfather fly. Weston remarked to Pamela, "It's too bad Grandpa can't fly like Daddy and Uncle Wayne!"

When this comment reached Smitty's ears, the famous Mudhole temper riled up and it was all the whole family could do to keep him from taking off immediately in the nearest airplane to show his grandchildren just how he could fly. He was grounded under doctor's orders, so the family prevailed on him to forget it. To soothe Smitty, they embarked on a program to enlighten the kids that Grandpa could, indeed, fly as well as Wayne and Kenny.

Pamela, Kenny's oldest daughter, went to school in Anchorage, and one day her teacher took the class to the Air Transportation Museum (which later burned down). Pam was looking at the old photographs when suddenly she exclaimed, "There's my grandpa!" Until that moment her teacher thought of her as another Smith, not the granddaughter of Mudhole Smith, the bush pilot. Now he understands why she wanted to become a test pilot.

During the late fifties and early sixties, some of the old-time pilots began getting together to form clubs for the purpose of "hangar flying" and general socializing. Smitty brought several of their conventions to Cordova. One club was called "QB" for Quiet Birdmen. The OX5 Club was limited to pilots who had flown airplanes equipped with the famous OX5 engine, which meant its members were really old-timers. At their reunions they could re-create the days when they all sat in the shade of a hangar or under the wing of a plane swapping yarns about flying. Back then it was part of the learning experience, but now it preserved the past.

Aviation Pioneers

"You had a tough pilot out of Cordova in Harold Gillam. But when Harold went to work for the Morrison-Knudsen Company at the beginning of the war, Mudhole Smith flew the mail from Fairbanks to Bethel, hitting all the way points in an old Pilgrim.

"We used to talk about how Gillam kept that old airplane right on schedule, regardless of weather. It was unbelievable what the man did. But when Smitty took over, I didn't see any difference. Same thing — he was just as tough and just as good as Harold Gillam was before him."

The words were those of Ray Petersen, president of Wien Consolidated Airlines and one of a whole galaxy of old-time bush pilots present in Cordova on April 28, 1973, to celebrate "Mudhole Smith Day." Others present were Jack Jefford, Jack Peck, Bob Reeve, Ray Petersen, John Cross, Sig Wien and Noel Wien. Also Jack Gannon, president of the Alaska OX5 Club; Pres Blatter, president of Alaska Airlines; Quentin DeBoer, old-time pilot and member of the Alaska Transportation Commission; Lanky Rice, executive vice-president of Wien Consolidated Airlines and former partner of Jack Peck; Doug Haynes, president of Alaska Aeronautical Industries, which flies the Kenai Peninsula; and Governor William A. Egan, Alaska's first elected governor and an early-day pilot.

The "hangar flying" was great and, as the pilots warmed up to perform verbal power dives on their old friend and "eyeball-to-eyeball" competitor, Mudhole was heard to observe that this would probably be "the Wounded Knee of bush pilots."

Some of the stories were amusing, some historic, and others just recalled old-time names from Alaskan aviation: Hans Mirow, Merle Sasseen, M.D. "Kirk" Kirkpatrick, and Harold Gillam, whose name is synonymous with tough flying.

Bob Reeve regaled the crowd with his own version of how Mudhole got his nickname: "Without that name," he asserted, "Smitty would be just another Smith, with no more entity than a hole in a doughnut! But now there are two famous Smiths in Alaskan history: "Soapy" Smith, the famous gunman of early Skagway, and "Mudhole" Smith, the famous pilot of early Cordova. I'll put Mudhole's name above Soapy's any day!"

The "Mudhole Smith Day" dinner was only one of a number of such events honoring Smitty. His name had not appeared in many of the books written on Alaskan bush pilots, and it was only about this time that Mudhole Smith's contributions were beginning to be recognized.

In 1977, Smitty was nominated to the Aviation Pioneers Hall of Fame, and I was invited to accompany him and Bertha to Latrobe, Pennsylvania, for the unveiling of the commemorative plaque.

Merle and Bertha Smith.

Latrobe is a little town in Pennsylvania, affectionately known as the "Birthplace of the OX5 Aviation Club." Fifteen aviation pioneers were to be honored by individual plaques on the Aviation Pioneers board.

The weather was beautiful in Latrobe until the night of the awards dinner in the Blue Angel dining room of the Latrobe airport. I should have known that even the weather could be counted on to make Mudhole Smith's award a memorable one.

The chaplain said a prayer: "The Lord is my pilot; I shall not perish. He maketh me to fly in clear skies. . . ."

The honors for the Hall of Fame sounded like a roster and history of aviation from the very beginning:

" . . . designer of . . ."

" . . . who was one of the earliest air examiners . . ."

" . . . three generations here . . ."

" . . . founder of. . . ."

When the Master of Ceremonies told of Mudhole's exploits, the high regard for Alaska bush pilots was clearly evident. He spoke of Mudhole's efforts to bring medical aid to fishermen and people in the bush, of flying in the toughest kind of weather and mountains, of his airlift which fed the town of Cordova for seven weeks. He told how Smitty was probably the first pilot to spot an enemy submarine in American waters in World War II.

All the while the clouds thickened and darkened outside the dining room window. When Mudhole Smith was introduced and stepped to the rostrum to speak, there immediately began a spectacular display of lightning behind his back. It seemed a most fitting welcome for Mudhole Smith to the OX5 Aviation Pioneers Hall of Fame.

Asked how he got his nickname, Mudhole told his audience: "Everyone wants to know how I got my name. Well, I'm not going to tell you! There's a writer here who's doing a book on me, and you'll just have to buy the book to find out!" The audience applauded.

The Aviation Pioneers Hall of Fame plaque was unveiled. It read:

Merle K. Smith
Was highly instrumental in developing aviation in Alaska.
Provided air service to remote villages, mines and camps.
Flew many tons of cargo from Canada to support U.S. Forces.
Conducted 136 mercy missions without pay or reward.
Flew more than 22,000 hours without injury to a passenger.
Inducted 1977.

That was certainly a condensation of his life. That's why some of what happened between the lines is told in this book.

———————

Mudhole Smith, pioneer Alaska flier, died in 1981 at the age of 73.